Financial Freedom for Beginners

How To Become Financially Independent and Retire Early

Nathan Bell

Disclaimer

All erudition contained in this book is given for informational and educational purposes only. The author is not in any way accountable for any results or outcomes that emanate from using this material. Constructive attempts have been made to provide information that is both accurate and effective, but the author is not bound for the accuracy or use/misuse of this information.

Table of Contents

CHAPTER ONE

Introduction To Financial Freedom

Guy and Tom are two friends who work together in a similar capacity under the same company. They both are alike and different, alike in the sense that they share the same responsibilities and duties, but different in their reactions and willingness to perform these duties. Guy is always ready to perform them, even when unforeseen circumstances arise; he is simply always prepared. However, Tom is the direct opposite; he is in a constant state of panic and crisis based on the complaint that he does not have enough funds to support these situations.

The subject of concern is, what creates this significant difference between these colleagues?

What Is Financial Freedom?

It is important to a lot of people or a vast majority of people that they can satisfy their needs or desire at whatever time it arises. However, many are not equipped with the mentality to actualise this desire; hence, the need for financial freedom.

The meaning of financial freedom is subjective to different people and the various situation they find themselves. For a teenager, financial freedom is independence from parents; it is them not having to depend on the income or allowances given by the parents. Therefore, teenagers might regard themselves financially free if they have their personal income which funds their lifestyle irrespective of the benefits provided by the parents. To a retiree, it is the freedom to have the desired lifestyle without the stress of bankruptcy because of the retirement plans or investments that have been set in place. To some people, it the ability to perform in a role they admire or remain self-employed without strain on their finances.

However, financial freedom, in general, refers to a lifestyle void of the concern or domination of income. In clear terms, it refers to the ability or status of a person to provide or support a need in whatever circumstance. It is a position where you are settled financially; any unplanned or sudden expense will not cause a dent to your financial state. It refers to a state of being economically independent without having to depend on salaries from employment. It is also important to note that financial freedom connotes a debt-free situation, that is; a person who wants to lay claim that he is financially free cannot claim that the money that funds his free state is from debt.

Financial freedom is not restricted to being able to only fund emergencies but also to find solace in the fact that your life after retirement has specific plans in place that would ensure financial stability and growth. It's a lifestyle that is dominated by money and a constant worry to make these funds.

It also entails the ability to retire early or quit a job simply because you have lost interest in that particular field but do not have a specific task that you are registered to at that specific time. It is the ability to afford a desired lifestyle without stress about the next paycheck. Therefore, you are in control of your finance and lifestyle instead of your financial state dictating a particular lifestyle it believes you can afford without collapse. It is the ability to work for cooperation or company based on the fact that you enjoy whatever role you are given and not because it is crucial to your finance.

The Means to Attain Financial Freedom

As stated in the above paragraphs, every individual seeks to attain financial independence and this state of finance has different meanings and interpretations to people. However, these people are expected to go through the same or similar steps to attaining financial freedom, hence, the reason for the subsequently discussed opinions;

- Set Goals: This is an essential principle to financial independence; every idea and investment needs motivation. Therefore, a set goal helps you to choose the right investment and employment options that would ensure you are moving towards a goal which leads to financial freedom. Also, these goals are advised to be in clear, specific and realistic forms because this would increase the possibility of achieving them. However, even after sustenance of a position where you no longer stress about money, has been reached, it is still important to live on or make a budget so that you do not overspend and return to your former stage. It is of primary importance to be purposeful about financial freedom.
- Make a Budget: it is vital to make a set budget; this would help to regulate your spending and ensure that the right percentage is invested in meeting your set goals. A budget is used to document the progress of savings and investments. This also helps to contain unplanned and unnecessary temptations to spend recklessly.

- Pay Loans: if you desire to have a financially independent lifestyle, it is essential to pay up or clear all loans; student loans, house loans or car loans. If this is not done, it would only consume or eat up the profits/interests of your investment. It is crucial to set up all financial investments on a fresh slate, so your desire for independence is not undermined by debt and the interests that overwhelm it.
- Register to an Automatic Savings Plan: There are various retirement savings plans made available for employees by their cooperation. For example; the 401(k)s made available for employees of private cooperation and Thrift Savings Plan available for federal government workers and members of the uniformed forces, gives individuals an option to have their savings automatically invested in a plan after their retirement. These plans contribute largely to financial freedom because of the matching contribution option that is contributed to your personal savings account and investment funds opportunities. Also, this particular option helps ensure that a specific percentage which has been registered by you is pulled from your salary and contributed to your investment before you start spending, and in some cases before tax deduction.
- Examine Investment Options: This is the central way to ensure financial freedom as every investment accommodates interest and growth based on the percentage and time it was contributed. It also provides individuals to choose an

investment option that suits their situation as there is a variety of them. However, it is advisable to begin investing as soon as because its success and growth are based on the time contributed and time fixed and decided to be for withdrawal. Therefore, it is essential to examine investment options or hire a financial advisor who could assist based on gathered knowledge to decide on an option for your situation. Growth can be supported with a weekly, monthly or yearly or any comfortably consistent plan that would not affect the individual's lifestyle but improve and manage the growth of savings.

- Accommodate Bargains: In most cases, when individuals begin to make some percentage of wealth, they decide that there is no point behind negotiating goods they can afford at the stated price. However, this a financial sucking idea which prevents a lot of people from saving expenses if they had asked for or agreed to a bargain price. This is so because they find it an injury and their status and would not like to appear cheap. Therefore, it is important to negotiate since this could save them a considerable amount of money if they submit themselves to negotiate with these sellers. Although some people refuse to negotiate because they believe that, some businesses are not open to negotiation, this might be in fact true, but some small-scale businesses are available to negotiate the price of goods. Also, buying in bulk and consistently from one seller attracts discounts and creates a more relaxed atmosphere to accommodate discounts.

- Be informed: knowledge in financial freedom is power. To reach and sustain a stage of financial independence, it is essential to keep yourself updated about economic laws, rules and regulations as they apply to you. Ensure that you are updated on the changes and improvement in tax laws and the investment and interest options; this would help ensure that your investment is not at a loss, and you profit at full capacity based on whatever option you choose to be reasonable and valuable to your desires. Also, it is an essential defence to avoid people who would like to delude an investor from making crucial investment options or cheat you from making the necessary profit. However, to prevent this, it is advisable to employ the services of an advisor.
- Do Not Spend More Than You Earn: This is of critical importance in every financial step or journey; it is also of vital importance to the course of financial freedom. Although the idea of financial freedom is to afford whatever lifestyle you desire without the fear of the impact it would make on your finance. It is also of notable importance to highlight "live below your means." An individual who is in a constant hurry to spend the funds or income that should be contributed to the savings of the financial freedom would find himself in a never-ending journey. This does not mean that you should cut down or limit your spending or cancel

spending at all, it merely projects the idea that an individual who is interested in financial freedom has to be able to distinguish between wants and needs. These needs have to be prioritised accordingly.

- Hire a Financial Advisor: In the preceding conclusions, it has been suggested that a financial advisor is needed; before and after the attainment of financial freedom. In cases, once individuals see that they have amassed so much wealth, they either invest or spend it wrongly, hence, the need to employ the services of an advisor. A financial advisor would help manage the wealth or funds that have been accumulated. An advisor could also be of help in ensuring that you subscribe to the right investment option and funds to minimise risks. Correspondingly, they help in determining a plan that would stabilise your freedom and also reasonable withdrawal plans for your situation.

Importance of Financial Freedom

It is the case that some people are not concerned about financial freedom, they are satisfied with the lifestyle of dependence on salaries and working for corporations because of their financial state, they are not concerned with the profits and interest from investing. However, apart from the benefits and advantages of financial independence, it also gives you the plan to schedule your day or time according to your desire. Your life is fixed with things that sincerely interest you. Therefore, you have the freedom of choice to select any of the following options;

There is no compulsion to work with or for a company, a financially free person has enough funds to identify a hobby as a job daily even though it might not provide as much as an actual job. The liberty to work based on the fact that you enjoy something rather than the necessity to fund your lifestyle.

It puts you in a relaxed and settled position or situation to do whatever you want. For instance, a financially free person who does not work for a company has the liberty and the funds to travel anywhere at any time without any impact on his status. However, someone else would have to apply for a break at the cooperation to attend to this. You have the liberty to plan your schedule and work at any time you desire. Financial Freedom does not only include being able to support your desired lifestyle. It also entails being able to assist and fund those who need this help.

Conclusively, the difference between Tom and Guy is that Guy has been able to identify with financial freedom to satisfy his needs while Tom is yet to recognise the steps and importance of this ideology.

action
plan
idea

CHAPTER TWO

Money Mindset Secret

What conviction do you have about money? Is it a sparse idea or commodity that cannot be attained after so much effort? Or are you of the belief that money is plentiful and the reality of being wealthy is a fact that is possible? Well, the opinion that you have, or support is referred to as a money mindset. It is merely your way of thinking or view when it comes to issues about money, funds, wealth and finance. It is of crucial importance in locking into financial freedom. A lot of people are not aware that they have a role in deciding what manifests in their life based on their thoughts and opinion, your money mindset goes a long way in determining the position of wealth you find yourself. This particular factor can be traced back to the connection between the law of attraction and the law of manifestation. These laws are the primary tools that come to play in issues concerning your money mindset and reality. The law of manifestation states that you attract the reality that you desire for yourself. The events that manifest in your life are attracted to the opinions you embody concerning a particular subject matter. Therefore, if you think that there is a scarcity of wealth and it cannot be acquired no matter the amount of hard work and skilfulness put into it, you might find your finance stagnant and in a position of destitute. It is essential to believe that money is obtainable for it to be the reality or manifestation in your life.

Therefore, the concept of money mindset refers to your belief and opinion about the circulation and existence of money or wealth in the world and your community. However, your money mindset is not shaped by the salary or allowances that you receive, and it is formed based on opinions that you have read, seen and experienced over the years. Sometimes, you unknowingly develop a money mindset without knowledge that it exists. Money mindset is an essential determining factor in attaining the status of financial freedom, your chosen position or mindset also determines your stand or orientation in issues concerning finance and economic changes; it reflects in your discussion and attitude towards others when a question about money is brought up. However, two underlying mindsets control the wealth or finance of every individual, and they are the abundance mindset and the scarcity mindset.

The abundance mindset refers to a state of belief or understanding that wealth and money can be acquired; that is, attaining money is a reasonable and possible idea that is not as distant or as far-fetched as many people believe. The abundance mindset puts people who identify with it in an available position to identify with financial freedom; the laws of attraction and manifestation are at an advantage in their lifestyle and finance. The people with the scarcity mindset, on the other hand, believe strictly in the thought that money is sparse, and attainment of money or wealth depends on a vigorous search which you cannot ascertain that money would be acquired after such search. In most cases, they find themselves working hard and with an urge or the constant need to acquire wealth but making little or less money compared to those with the abundance mindset. It is important to note that a particular mindset is not dependant on the money you currently have but on a series of event and the conclusion you have unconsciously or unconsciously drawn; this is the reason for the possibility that some millionaires or head of offices are encompassed with the scarcity mindset. It could be as a result of various events, and it affects their investments negatively because of the fear it instils about risks. However, this does not mean that once an individual has identified with a particular mindset, he would solely depend on it for life. The remedies are some of the issues discussed in this chapter.

The important question at this point is how your money mindset is chosen or decided? The mindset you seem to identify or select is as a result of various factors. An individual might want to identify with either the abundance or scarcity mindset as a result of some situations or ideas highlighted in the combination of your personal choices, sometimes your unconscious thoughts or feelings made this choice a long time ago before you become aware of the existence of a money mindset. It is sometimes caused by the financial circumstances or situation an individual grew up with, a person whose parents or family were in constant disarray because of limited funds or unstable finance would probably identify with the scarcity mindset, to such person, attaining funds will always be a struggle rather than a pleasurable act.

Also, the economic or the financial state of the general public during an individual's growth is a factor in determining one's mindset. For instance, if Tom's community or country was in recession during his formation years, he believes and absorbs the ideology that there is little or not enough money to benefit the entire population. The money mindset is majorly determined during the childhood or growing stage because most opinions and ideologies are formed during these years.

The Effects of Your Mindset on Money

Sometimes people find themselves in favourable situations where money is always available to support every need and desire that arises. However, most people do not belong to this particular category. Whether an individual acknowledges it or not, the amount or percentage of money that you make or that you have in your account is as a result of the mindset you have subscribed. Therefore, it is essential to understand the importance and the effect of the money mindset so that it could be changed if it is identified as the factor of detriment on your road to financial freedom, and if this is not the case, it is essential to continue the abundance money mindset to attain and sustain a financially free state.

What are the effects of money mindset on your current financial state?

- It helps nurture financial freedom: a good (abundance) money mindset helps to attain the position of economic freedom and independence. Beyond achieving financial freedom is sustaining it and growing in a financially free state. This mindset helps to ensure that there is a manifestation of wealth and growth in your reality rather than the scarcity mindset, which would limit the wealth and funds received.
- It limits financial growth: the scarcity mindset is a massive barrier for growth. A person with a scarcity

mindset does not necessarily have to be without funds, he could be wealthy to some extent, but he does not have any desire or curiosity to become aware of what exists beyond his current financial state. Therefore, a scarcity mindset could make individual comfortable in a position where he should ordinarily want to change or move beyond, as change is expected to be the only constant procedure in every individual.

- It determines your approach to money-related issues: A determinant in the way you talk, spend, live, and opinions you give in every situation about finance or any other subject matter is based on your mindset. As stated earlier, a person with a scarcity mindset would identify no reason or importance in making more funds or profit. However, an abundantly conscious person tends to identify the most valuable positions and ideas in a room so that he could invest and promote such a financial situation.
- It affects your business dealings: take, for instance, a situation where you would like to meet an investor to invest in your business or cooperation but your scarcity mindset that does not have total confidence in the idea that you are presenting. Most individuals find confidence attractive, and no one would like to invest funds in a business that the CEO feels has an indifferent feeling concerning. Therefore, it is not enough to stand between

the scarcity and abundance mindset, to be financially free; an individual must choose abundance and be most confident in his choice.

- A scarcity mindset might be interfering with your goals and limiting your potential. Due to your constant fear of loss or "not having enough", many profitable business deals are not considered because an individual with a scarcity mindset is never ready to take risks. They are unaware of the fact that every investment growth or profit is made based on the ability to take chances on reasonable or potential business deals.
- An abundance mindset gives you an edge: it allows you to see and identify opportunities in situations or cases where others believe there is only limited profit. It gives you foresight because of the belief that benefit would be made in whatever situation or account that you invest. Therefore, you are more open compared to others with the scarcity mindset when it comes to investing in new ideas or businesses.

Your money mindset determines a lot of factors in your life; it determines your association, the places and events you attend, your response to issues and every other aspect of life

Steps to Attaining the Abundance Mindset.

You do not have to live in a loss for the rest of your life if you have been a victim of the scarcity mindset for some time. A scarcity mindset can be clarified when your lifestyle and expenses are based on your paycheck and amount of salary or income you get. With such a mindset, you might never have the ability or fierceness to participate in whatever interests because of the fear that you do not or will never have enough.

However, the abundance mindset is filled with various advantageous options and opportunities, and it considers every profit or advantage that could be acquired from investment deals which have been ignored or avoided by individuals with a scarcity mindset. A person with an abundance mindset would never consider the possibility that a business or investment might not be successful at its start-up stage; they are optimists when it comes to issues, ideas and thoughts that concern money. There are some necessary steps to shift from the position of scarcity to abundance to ensure financial freedom; identify your current mindset: to grow or move on from a particular mindset, it is important to own up to and acknowledge one's current stage of belief to proceed further. You have to be self-aware and conscious of this change or development, to ensure that you are mindful of the shift from scarcity to abundance.

- Research: If you are reading this, you have taken the first and most important step in shifting to the abundance mindset. It is essential to identify what kind of mindset you identify with by reading books and carrying out research on different money mindsets.

- Focus on benefits not losses: although most mindsets are formed during childhood or the teenage years, in some cases, it is formed during adulthood when you have a job. It is even possible that you grew with an abundance mindset, but due to some losses during your adult stage, there was a loss that sabotaged your entire belief of abundance. How then do you move forth from this? To grow beyond the scarcity mindset, it is of importance to identify the factor that established it in the first instance and move beyond this affair or circumstance. Therefore, it is important to focus on the profits that can be made when the loss has been forgone. Let go of every mistake that has been made in your finances to establish to release negativity and harbour positive energy.
- Budget: in every stage and decision towards attaining financial freedom, it is crucial to identify a direction or budget for the money made. A budget is a laid-out plan of funds that is spent on every aspect of an individual's life. How then does a budget contribute to the abundance mindset? It is essential to understand that saving or working for money without a significant plan can be aggravating when you believe you do not have any use for the wealth garnered. A budget is like a motivator that

would give you a definite reason to identify with abundance. From the standpoint of a marketer, if he does not have a particular task or purpose of attaining money, he would feel indifferent about his financial situation, which resembles the scarcity mindset.

- Associate yourself with people of a similar mindset: in most cases, individual energy or esteem is drawn from those he surrounds or associates himself with; it is essential to associate yourself with people that identify with the abundance mindset to be of abundance. For development in every stage of life or a particular aspect, it is vital to consort people who have gotten this position right, to learn the appropriate procedures; fraternise with the right kind of people. In this case, it entails associating with other people who can be pinpointed to have the abundance mindset or similar values that you would like to assimilate.
- Reaffirm yourself: it is essential to have motivations or goals that would affirm the advantages and needfulness of the abundance mindset.
- Take note of your finances: it is important to have a ritual of examining the income and spending of your account, this would assist in sustaining your financial mindset; every individual grows based on the fact that whatever they have invested in has made some percentage of income.

- Avoid complaining: most individuals find themselves complaining about the circulation of money; this only contributes and hardens the scarcity mindset. Therefore, you have to avoid all negative positions and thoughts to ensure that there is no contributing factor to a scarcity mindset. As this is mindfully done, it establishes growth for an abundance mindset. Create a ritual to show gratitude to yourself, appreciate whatever stage of growth you have been able to attain.

To achieve financial freedom, it essential that this necessary change or step is carried out as it determines the profit and investment choices that an individual would be able to make. Disregard the opinion that some people are born with the abundance mindset; hence, their success and growth in finance; take note that your thoughts and ideas about money are something you can manage. You should be in charge of your money mindset rather than taking the principal role in your lifestyle.

CHAPTER THREE

Passive Income

Every individual has that one friend who is not interested in going through the stress of taking a job that would require a strict work ethic; you might not even have a friend as you are that person to someone else. Every person reaches that stage in life where no ideas or job are of possible interest to them, the only task they seem to enjoy or consider enjoyable are those that require little or no effort from them. In the technological era that the world has evolved into, most people are interested in the strenuous jobs that require total dedication and adherence to schedules or rules that do not fit their desires.

What is Passive Income?

Passive income refers to the money or salary gotten from a task or "job" you are not actively involved. Unlike any other job or income gotten, the passive income does not require a significant level of effort to attain or sustain the situation. As far as there is a passive income, there would surely be an active income, which differentiates these categories of income. The active income involves and requests active use of time and effort to generate income while the former does not. However, there is an advanced level of passive income which is referred to as the progressive income; it relates to income sustained by enforcing little or minimal effort into performing required tasks. Then, what advantage is gotten from passive income? The most obvious advantage and benefit of passive income is the fact that it exerts little or no energy from its participants; you are getting paid for doing activities and tasks that do not require your physical participation. However, some passive income tasks might be a bit demanding at its initial stage, but it becomes easy after. The basic principle of this idea is to earn while you do nothing. An example of this is rental property income. The second benefit is the tax option available under this decision; some taxing institutions distinguish between the different types of income and tax them appropriately, not generally.

In this objective, there are three main categories of income as recognised by the Internal Revenue Service (IRS), they are passive income, active income and portfolio income. According to the IRS, the passive income is gotten from three categories, which are trade, rental and passive activities which you do not significantly participate. The primary streams to generate passive income are through investment, real estate, trading, and blogging. Individuals who subscribe to this are usually huge supporters on self-employment rather than formal jobs. The subject of self-employment is the significant connection it has to financial freedom.

How Can Passive Income Be Generated?

If you have suddenly quit your job or you've been fired and plan to depend on your savings, it is only a matter of time before this savings finish. Even if you do not belong to any of these categories, but you desire to earn more than your salary, a passive income is an important aspect to be considered. You do not have to be necessarily jobless to make money passively; it could be regarded as a side hustle to enhance your financial status when added to your basic pay. The following are some of the ways passive income can be generated;

Although people project the passive income as profit acquired "while you sleep", this is a false representation of the entire idea of passive income. This particular community or set of people fail to identify or present the main constitute of passive marketing which involves the fact that you must have put in a specific percentage of work at the initial stage of the project. Either time or money has been greatly invested to finally put you in the position where you can earn "while you sleep." This mentality misleads people into delving into passive income without any necessary training or investment in their knowledge of the subject matter. Therefore, a lot of work has to be generated into the start-up to ensure a properly managed income.

Passive income entails contribution, without this, where is profit gotten? To ensure that you would consistently enjoy a healthy profit from financial income. It is important to note that that you would have to invest something in the idea that would generate this income. It could be time or money, depending on the business you decide to invest. Take, for instance, investment in dividend stocks; investment in dividend stocks exists in companies that pay a particular percentage of their profit to their shareholders or investors. To qualify for an idea like this, you must have invested a large amount of money in becoming a shareholder in that company. Also, an investment in real estate would require a substantial investment in funds and time in finding a property that would produce a large percentage of income. Therefore, profit is gotten from the rental of these properties.

Therefore, to generate a particular percentage of income through passive income, it is essential to understand that no money is earned fully. Although this might some seem to be the case since you have that friend that does nothing but looks to make a lot, you have to understand that some principles and effort has been laid down at a point in his passive income career for him to identify with this position.

Steps to Attaining Passive Income

Due to the discussion in previous pages, you have become familiar with some of the importance and measures to attaining a stable passive income. However, it is necessary to state these steps in clear and precise terms to ensure that every participant establishes a well-thought passive income that would provide him consistent profit in the long-term. It is possible to invest into passive income at a loss after the investment of time and money, to avoid this, it is vital to highlight and define the reasonable steps to be taken by anyone interested in passive income as an actual job or a side job.

- It is essential to have an idea: it is not strange to you at this point to learn that passive income provides you with a lot of options. However, it is crucial to research every opportunity and select the most suitable one. Interest is an essential factor in passive income; since you are expected to invest your time and money. If interest is absent at this point, you might become tired or weary while your profit takes time to grow. Therefore, in choosing your idea, you have to consider several factors that apply to your particular situation and the money you have in hand. If you have a significant capital to invest, real estate or dividend stock investment is a desirable option for you. Although you may not get the profit and interest at the exact time of contribution, the profit you would make after you have given the investment time to grow is incomparable to that contribution. Some of the ideas that can be considered by any participant are;

- Selling information: the technological stage that the world has reached has made the sale of products that contain specific information possible. Most people have become curios, highly to learn things; hence, the massive production in the information provided products, for example, e-books and audiobooks. Once the set-up process or effort to write a book has been covered, it is left to the participants to earn money while products are sold. However, to gain from this, you have to ensure that your products are not mediocre as there is a lot of competition in this aspect.
- Rental: although this idea might seem traditional to some people, real estate investment and ownership of property is an excellent way to make passive income. It does not exert as much effort as the above idea, but it requires understanding in the process and technique of real estate to avoid the loss of capital that has been invested. An individual who is familiar with the components and requirements of passive income through real estate investment can establish this idea as a reasonable and actionable source of income after retirement. According to John Graves who is an Accredited Investment Fiduciary, there are three requirements that must be

satisfied to ensure the stability of passive income; you must be able to determine the profit you expect from the contribution made to the investment, you must have an idea of the total cost of the property and the expense required and also the financial risks that accompany owning the property as this factors would prepare you for every situation.

- Affiliate marketing: this might not produce as much profit as the already stated ideas, but it is a way of earning without inputting so much effort. What is affiliate marketing? It is a marketing technique whereby bloggers or marketers promote the products of a third party by posting the links to such products. How does this technique make money for you? If an affiliate link is posted on your site and a consumer clicks on the link, at this moment, purchasing products from the third party, you are entitled to a commission from the third party. The percentage gotten solely depends on the number of products that are purchased. However, success in passive income through affiliate marketing might take some effort because you would need to develop an audience for your site and create a stable percentage with consistent and reasonable content.
- Lending: Peer-to-peer lending involves lending money to people through a registered third party. The profit made

from this idea is on the interest paid by the party that has been lent money.

    - Dividend stocks, High-interest savings account, Rent out an extra room or car, Display Ads

- Create a goal board: this is more of personal use to you than the business. It is not going to be easy to participate in passive income. However, it is essential to note the idea where you would like to invest, the profit rates of that idea, the percentage of contribution you would like to make and the profit expected at the time of return. It is essential to set these goals as it helps to motivate you during the time of discouragement; hence, it is most important to set your goals on paper. Studies have shown that goals written out by individuals become more actionable and reasonable to them than the ones that exist in their minds. Therefore, write out your goals and expound as much as you can on paper as this would assist in your investment.
- Plan your decisions and steps: after an idea and goal, the next step is to plan your choices and decisions to achieve these goals. Note, the decisions and necessary options that you will need to consider getting from one position in your goal plan to the next. Making plans for your goals at every single point would make them more realistic and actionable to you and everyone who might consider assisting you. Therefore, it is important not to set goals

arbitrarily and to understand what would be required from you to get to your desired stage of earning passively.

- Create an alternative plan: there are different situations; passive income could be some people's backup while some depend solely on passive income. To attain financial freedom, you cannot be dependent on only one source of income. Innovation is key. You have to invest and create other plans while you set actionable goals to reach a stable stage of passive income, the reason for this is that some passive income ideas are not usually successful all the time despite the time and money invested in it. It is merely the nature of the business, and this is the reason for the importance of knowledge and research on whatever topic you decide to invest. Therefore, if you plan to invest in dividend stock or start a blog, these ideas do not require you to quit your day job and depend solely on them. Instead, it is advisable not to be dependent on these businesses to have a reckless financial situation.
- Connect with successful people in that area: the importance of networking cannot be overemphasised. If you desire to become successful in a particular field, an essential idea or option is to investigate or research on those who have made significant income from such an approach. Apart from reading about them, it is important to connect and talk to these people to create an understanding of the requirements and the expectations

you should have about a particular system. In every step of your relationship with them, it is important always to find the things they are doing that you are yet to integrate into your business ideas and goals. Inquire about their ideas and strategies and implement it as it may apply to your passive income situation.

Benefits of Passive Income

It quickens your financial freedom status by adding an extra stream of income to double the percentage of the contribution made to your savings. It helps to widen or eliminate the limit that has been put in place to control or restrict a particular budget plan. This also helps to actualise the reasonability behind the concept of a money mindset, as you are more conscious and have faith in plans or ideas when there are ideas placed in motion to project the basic principle.

Participants have an option to retire early, quit their job to participate in something they are genuinely interested. Some individuals are unable to apply to or participate in situations that they desire because those jobs might not earn them much, and their regular job is time-consuming. The passive income job allows them to participate in their desired position and make more than or close to the percentage gotten from active jobs.

It is an advantageous technique set in place for a situation where an individual suddenly loses his job. Many cooperation and businesses have to urgently let some workers go before the end of their contract due to various reasons. Many of these workers are in disarray at the loss of their jobs. This does not have to be the situation as you are not primarily affected in the time that exists during the loss of employment and the acquisition of another.

It creates an alternative plan for funds or income after retirement. Many workers are dependent on their Thrift Savings Plans and 401(k)s without considering the possibility that an emergency which could clear out these savings could arise. A retired individual interested in passive income, mainly, rental activities could rely or depend on the salary gotten from this source.

However, an individual who plans to contribute to this must have the virtue of patience. Every option available to generate passive income requires patience as a person cannot get wealthy or financially free from this income overnight. Therefore, an individual who is willing to remain patient overtime can be successful and attain financial freedom through any of the option offered by passive income.

It allows personal growth, a daily or permanent routine at a particular job can become repetitive, unnecessary and limiting. Passive income provides you with an option to add a new business idea that aids your financial and intellectual growth. Apart from this, it gives a lot of spare time to participate in activities that genuinely interest you at whatever desired time.

Not every individual appreciates his current job, and not all would attain financial freedom from their current jobs. Therefore, to hasten your attainment of the financial freedom status, it is essential to indulge the passive income ideas.

CHAPTER FOUR

Dividend Investing

Any individual who seeks to earn through passive income has to understand and appreciate the importance and strategy that involves dividend stock investment. One of the characteristics of financial freedom highlighted in previous chapters is the fact that you might not have to work with or for anybody to identify with the financially free status. Dividend stocks investing is one of the most profound ways to attain financial freedom and passive income. It offers a chance to earn a massive percentage of income apart from the regular gotten from your daily job. It involves getting profit from the value of the market you invested by buying shares.

What is Dividend Investing?

Dividend investing is an investment or passive income option that offers company or business shareholders a percentage of income or profit based on the investment made towards that particular business. Usually, the distribution of profit to shareholders can be paid in cash or into a reinvestment plan, and this could also be paid by increasing or handing out more shares to the individual instead of a cash payment made to the bank. Through dividend payments, a company or business dedicates a percentage of its profit to shareholders, and the other portion is devoted to the growth of the market to ensure a stable cycle of profit. There is no compulsion to pay dividends to shareholders or stockholders, it is merely the choice of the management to fund the benefit of their share through two primary options; with cash by depositing it to their account or the opportunity to reinvest it in the company's shares. However, there is no general rule to decide when dividends should be paid; this is determined based on the requirement and situation of each cooperation. In dividend investing, it is essential to be careful about the time you choose to invest and be critical of the cooperation or business you decide to invest; this is of notable warning especially to high-income investors. Every individual who decides to contribute or participate in dividend investing has to ensure that the company of interest is in a stable financial state, that is, there is an increase in stock rate, high production of reliable product or services and there is potential for growth in the products, company and management of such business. The opinion of dividends presented by each individual is subjective to their experience; dividends are good or bad depending on your investment strategy or approach. For profit to be paid to shareholders on the company's level, the management team agrees on a percentage of profit or gain that should be given or paid to the investors and that which should be reinvested in the company's stock, however, this decision by the management is merely a suggestion as it requires confirmation from the board of directors. After this procedure, the company is expected to announce the dividend rate, and payment is made to the shareholders.

It is important to note that dividend investing is meant for people of various groups, although some people might argue that dividend investing applies only to or it is only suitable for retirees, this is not the truth about this investment option.

Types of Dividends

In regular investing, the investor is not entitled to a percentage of profit; however, in dividend investing, the investor or shareholder is expected to be paid a particular interest of the capital invested. Furthermore, this payment is not restricted to a specific model; it does not have to be only cash payment. A company is allowed to pay an investor with cash, assets or an option to reinvest. The model of payment is left to the investor to choose, or not if the mode of payment or profit was clearly defined in the stock quote. Companies or businesses are allowed to make payment to their investors through any of the options discussed below:

- Payment by cash: The most known payment of dividends is by cash. These companies or businesses pay the profit of the investor's interest or dividends with money. The payment by cash mode entails the transfer and payment of cash or funds from the company's account to the investor's account; this does not confirm the idea that money can only be paid to the investor through a wired transfer. In some cases, the profit of the stock or investment is paid in cash.
- Payment by stock: stock refers to the total money or income that a company has gathered from shares bought by investors or shareholders. How then do you pay shareholders profit with stock? This particular payment is

made by reinvesting their profit to purchase more shares in the company. It is mostly done in companies that offer the option of a Dividend Reinvestment Plan (DRIP) to investors. So, instead of converting their profit into cash and making transfers to their account, their benefit is further invested in purchasing more shares and increasing the profit that they would eventually get from their original investment.

- Payment by assets: In some instances, shareholders might not be interested in gaining cash or more shares as profit, especially in the case of companies that have a decline in their overall profit. They might not even have the ability to pay in cash due to this reason. Hence, the availability of payment by assets, no company is restricted to cash and shares payment alone. A company may pay with assets like real estate and investment securities.
- In some very uncommon situations, a company might decide to pay a "special" dividend. The special dividend is the kind of profit paid outside your regular contract of payment (regular contract of payment could refer to annual or quarterly payments.) The "special" amount is usually as a result of an extra boost in the total profit made by the company or business.
- There are other modes of the payment depending on the company invested in; an investor can be paid with shares

a new company established by the original company invested.

Steps to Investing in Dividend Stocks

How do you ensure that you have gone through the right process to invest? What impact does dividend investing have on your financial status? What is the connection between financial freedom and dividend investing? These are some of the issues discussed in this section.

- Research: in every area of finance, research is vital to ensure that an individual is investing in a goal; profit, not a loss. To ensure that you invest in a reliable cooperation that pays a profit of shares to shareholders, it is essential to identify a company with high-quality products and a large company with financial stability. These sorts of companies are with the highest probability of paying dividends as they already have a stable financial status and capital to handle problems in the economy that might affect the profit, progress and finance of the entire company. They have enough experience to understand the right procedure and techniques that should be put in place. Also, the large accomplished companies are the best to invest in because they are aware of and practice other modes of maximising the shareholder's wealth. For instance, companies in the pharmaceutical's sector, oil and gas and banks are known to have stable dividend-paying platforms as people are always interested and in need of healthcare products and financial services. The best position to start your research is to create a list or identify the company or cooperation that appear or have been reported to have a stable financial status. After this, it is advisable to highlight the cooperation that you are interested in buying stocks. Also, ensure that you have enough funds to invest in such company to become a shareholder because a large part of being a shareholder is investing funds that help to build or support the financial state of a company or cooperation.

- Study the stock quote: the stock quote is the summary of the information of a company an individual should be aware of before investing. Therefore, if you are unsure about the stand of a company on the payment of dividends or to learn about the options available for dividend payments, the stock quotes should be considered to familiarise yourself with the policies of dividends payments of each company.
- Purchase the stock: once you have successfully carried out research and identified the company or business, you would like to invest. The next reasonable step is to purchase the shares of stock. This can be done personally by you to the company or through a broker. A broker is a mediator or an intermediary between a buyer and seller; therefore, a broker, in this case, acts a middle man between you and the management of the company you choose. However, not all companies offer the option to buy stocks directly through the company; some necessitate the requirement of purchase through a brokerage company or institution. Some businesses even require that a minimum investment between

$25 to $500 is made if an individual desire or insists on buying stock directly through the company. To avoid this, an individual would have to register with a brokerage institution, or if it is the case that the company does not offer the option to purchase stock directly, the individual would still have to register. Some brokerage institutions or firms are Ally Investment. eTrade and TD Ameritrade.

- Subscribe to DRIP (Dividend Reinvestment Plan): in dividend investing, you have two options to attaining your profit; a cash payment into your bank account or reinvestment. To ensure the sustenance of financial freedom and independence, it is important to be a participant or to be registered under DRIP. This plan is an automatic investment plan that ensures that profit that could have been converted into cash and sent to your account is reinvested into more shares. It is most advisable to enrol in DRIP to ensure that an individual's finance grows with the companies. To subscribe to this reinvestment option, an individual has to contact their broker if registered by one.
- Keep tabs on your dividends: companies are not entitled to pay shareholders. It is a choice rather than a requirement. The implication of this is that companies or businesses can choose to eliminate, increase or reduce their dividends at any given time. Therefore, when you are always aware of the changes and progress made to your dividends by tracking your brokerage account, you can conclude if the percentage

of profits has fallen below standard and decide the ideal time to sell your stock or shares.

Benefits Of Dividend Investing

After the necessary procedures of dividend investing has been complied with, it is important to ensure that an individual adopts a reasonable strategy in ensuring the growth of the stock. It is essential to diversify investment across different sectors or companies if it can be afforded. This is to ensure that the investment of an individual is not dependent on only one industry creating a crash or accident if there are any financial fluctuations to the company or that particular sector of the company. In the same vein, it is advisable to invest in companies or businesses across the world to avoid dependence on one specific government. Therefore, you can make a profit from different companies and avoid reliance on a particular government. There are various advantages to investing in the dividend investment option;

- It serves as a steady means of passive income: as established in the previous chapter of this book, passive income is significant to your financial status in life. It is necessary to have a side-job that provides a passive income in attaining financial freedom in some cases. In this situation, dividend investing is a beneficial kind of way to achieve passive income. This particular type involves a substantial investment of money to become a shareholder and you are entitled to income or profit as far as you remain a shareholder. This specific example of earning passive income is particularly attractive to retirees or people close to the retirement stage; it ensures that the retired does not have a significant a particular role in the company and they do not have to exert so much energy in attaining their income.

- Retainment of ownership: In some situations, an investment can be frustrating, primarily when you have invested in a company that does not pay dividends because all your profit is tied to stock. Therefore, the only way to access this profit is to sell your shares, as a result of this, forfeiting your percentage of ownership of shares of the company. This is not the case in investment in dividend stocks. Investment in dividend stocks gives the option to retain your percentage of ownership of shares as a shareholder while you attain the profit of the shares owned.
- Substantial profit: there is a higher level or percentage of gain available in dividend investment, unlike other types of investments. For instance, when you purchase a particular portion in shares of a company that does not pay shareholders profit, you that exact number of shares. However, in dividend investing, you are a given the option to either reinvest the profit of your shares to buy more or for it to be deposited into your account. There is no requirement that you withdraw funds from your

account to buy more shares when you can easily reinvest profit from your current stocks to purchase more.

Payment of dividends seems to be a loss on the part of the company or business paying the profit of shares to investors. Therefore, why do these companies indulge the option of dividends when its not a compulsion or an issue of legality for them? No reason can be generally applied to all companies to be regarded as their reason for this. However, every company has a right peculiar to its situation.

Dividends help to sustain trust, although the companies do not have to pay for the profit of shares. They decide to do this to honour the expectations and desire of the investor. A company that pays robust and consistent dividends is more likely to attract a more substantial capacity of investors willing to invest than one that does not honour the desire of the public. The payment of dividends to investors portrays a positive financial image and status of the company. Dividends help to attract investors or shareholders. A starting company that can secure a substantial percentage of quality products which does not have enough capital or investors in assisting its establishment can declare a level of dividend. This declaration helps to attract potential investors into examining the profits that could be gained by them if they choose to invest in a particular business or company. The interest of potential investors can assist in growing the stock value of such company. Therefore, the companies, in most cases, need the help of the investors to grow their businesses, and these investors need the companies to increase their funds or money by offering them the opportunity to invest in their shares. Also, dividends help to reduce the impact of a financial fluctuation or disability of the stock market on the investors, as a result of this reducing the risk of loss.

How does Dividend Investing Secure Financial Freedom?

The main idea of this book is to help individuals ensure a financially free state. So, having discussed and understood the discipline of dividend investing, how does this particular feature contribute to the attainment of financial freedom?

Dividends investing helps to grow and expand financial status. The extra income gotten from the profit of income invested by shareholders helps to establish an expansion of profits. When you subscribe to dividend investing, it helps to build an independent financial state due to substantial growth in profit or interest over time. Also, unlike stock that does not have a stable financial state in most situations and they do not guarantee a profit, the dividend stocks offer a partial profit on the capital invested.

Conclusively, apart from the idea of rental estates highlighted in the previous chapter, dividend investing is another stable way to achieve financial freedom and independence. It is most reliable because it gives participants an option to sell their shares if the dividend of a particular company reduces or if it loses sustainable profit in the investor's opinion.

CHAPTER FIVE

Stock Investments

At this point, you have become familiar with the topic of stock. However, if you have skipped the definition of stock in previous chapters, this is another opportunity to familiarize yourself with the issue of stock. Unlike the previous chapters, the topic, benefits, steps and strategy of stock investment to benefit a stable and significant profit would be discussed.

What Is Stock Investing?

Stock refers to the percentage of shares allocated to a particular individual who has invested a significant portion of money in becoming a shareholder or investor of a specific company. These investors purchase stocks or shares in a company that they believe would contribute to their financial status with an increase in the value of their product and stock. A stock is a sort of investment in the ownership of a company; giving you a percentage of the ownership rights of a company. In simple words for more understanding, stock investing is purchasing shares or a portion of a company to sustain a financial status or receive a substantial amount of profit in the case of companies that allocate dividends. Apart from an increase in the economic situation of the investor, what do companies gain from investment in stocks? Why would any company want to share their right of ownership with an individual by allowing them to invest in their business or company? There are a lot of factors attributed to this. However, the most suitable answer is their need to multiply profit of products and to raise capital for the establishment of their business or company and also ensure a constant level of funds to operate their venture. Any individual who owns a particular percentage of shares is referred to as an investor or shareholder, an individual who holds this position is entitled to a substantial share of the profits made from the products of such company. Take, for instance, an individual who purchases about 200 shares of a company which has 1000 shares in total, that person holds claim to the ownership of 20% of such company's profit. Therefore, a shareholder or investor cannot be regarded to be the sole owner of a company; they only own a percentage of the company that their shares covers. How then are the shares to be sold accessed? Companies of the public broadcast the message of their desire to sell through the stock markets and this sale is further confirmed on such platforms applied to, an example of a stock market platform is the New York Stock Exchange. Through, this chapter, there would be an elaboration of things that should be understood and considered as basics for anyone interested in stock investment. It is essential to understand the basics of stock investing as it would serve as a guide to assist in ensuring the success of an individual's experience in the stock exchange. As the general issue in finance, nothing is permanent, and there are constant fluctuation and decrease in any issue that may concern stock investment; hence, the importance of the basic principles of stock investment discussed through this chapter. They are dedicated to ensuring that you are equipped with the right ideas and opinions that would assist in managing any issue or subject of stock investment. Among the many principles presented in this chapter is the need to ensure your investment is well-spread. No rule restricts you or constrains you to a particular company for investment. Therefore, the increase and development of the number of companies invested in cushioning the effects and failures on your finance. For instance, if A invested all his money in company Z, and B invested all his money in company Y and some other companies, sharing the funds invested. B would not be as affected as A who has focused all his funds on a particular company, causing a breakdown if there is a decrease in the profit made by Company Z or if such a company becomes bankrupt. Having stated the importance and the need to invest in stocks, how then do you make money from stock investments?

How to Invest In Stocks

Although many individuals claim to be wildly interested in the topic of stock investment. They are not able to act upon these desires because they lack the knowledge to make necessary procedures to make these desires a reality; the desire being 'stock investing.' Therefore, it is important to highlight and define the right steps to ensure you are in alignment with the proper procedures to stock investing.

Identify your mode of purchase, in stock investing; you have the option to either purchase your shares or stocks through the company/brokerage or as an individual. Each of these options has unique features and opportunity; therefore, you would have to identify the option best suitable for your condition. Every company does not offer individual purchase; however, the companies that do offer it in some cases might insist on a minimum investment between $25 to $100. Therefore, it is advisable to register with a brokerage company; open a brokerage account. The process of opening a brokerage can be compared to the simplicity of opening a statement with the bank. The percentage charged on your profit or value by the brokerage company is not fixed, hence the importance to consider every option possible.

Basic Principles in Stock Investing

To ensure that your stock investment journey is a smooth sail towards financial freedom, it is essential to highlight and define some basic principles that guide the stock market. Also, you would be introduced to the dynamics of the stock market; its procedures and functions and how to manage some of the situations you might find yourself in as a stock market investor.

In stock investing, every shareholder needs to understand that they only own a percentage of the shares that make up the company, they do not have a right or entitlement to the assets that are held by the cooperation, company or firm. Therefore, you can not claim to own the totality of a company as an investor or shareholder. An investor or shareholder can not make decisions that may affect or concern the company by himself or subjectively. Therefore, a shareholder can not leave the company with confidential documents without the necessary authorization even with the claim or opinion to carry out an action that would benefit the company because the company owns the materials, not the shareholder; the document is in the company's name. This is known as the principle of separation of ownership and control.

Furthermore, the ownership of stocks in a particular company gives you the right and opportunity to vote on issues that concern the finance and welfare of the company during shareholder meetings. It gives you the right to receive a percentage of the company's profits; which are referred to as dividends if it is included to be a feature of the company in their stock quote. This principle also gives you the opportunity or liberty to sell personal shares at any time and to any individual of your choosing. The issue of not being able to make decisions for the company or cooperation is not regarded as a problem by most shareholders, as far as they are attributed to the right percentage of the company's profits. Therefore, if an investor desires an increased rate of profit compared to whatever is acquired, such an investor needs to increase the percentage of shares purchased in that company.

However, for individuals who own a higher percentage of stocks or shares than most people, they have a higher level of control and voting power in the company when compared to other shareholders who own less. The authority or power that your vote carries marginalizes based on the percentage of shares allocated to you. Also, for individuals who own a large portion of the company's stock, they are given the authority to choose individuals who make up the company's board of directors; this obligation is most evident in the case in which a company buys out another company. You do not buy only a percentage of shares in this situation; new management owns the entire company. Therefore, the new administration is given the liberty to choose a new league of the board of directors. The newly elected board is saddled with the responsibility of reelecting new executives or professionals that would ensure an increase in the value and profit of the cooperation. Managers and Chief Executive Officers (CEOs) are usually among the newly elected executives.

In stock investing, every individual is offered two significant types or options of stock to invest in; they are the common and preferred stock. Therefore, any intending investor has to choose the type of stock that would be invested. However, before this choice can be made, as it is one that should be made wisely and carefully, an individual has to understand the provisions of each type of stock. These divisions are subsequently discussed below:

- Common stock: generally, when the issue of stocks is being discussed, it usually refers to common stocks. This particular division of stock investing gives the investor or shareholder an entitlement or opportunity to vote on issues that concern the company during shareholders' meetings. Individuals who invested this kind of stocks are entitled to receive dividends of their investment if they have invested in a company which pays investors. Also, the investors in this category are entitled to elect the board of directors. However, in the hierarchy of priorities, and in the case whereby an unbalanced financial state of a company is present, the common stock investors are at the bottom. In the case of a liquidation, the common stock shareholders only have rights to the remaining assets or profits after the bondholders, or preferred stockholders have been issued their share of profit and assets, this particular principle of the common stock can be regarded as a risk on the investors

- Preferred stock: the division of preferred stock does not offer the entitlement to vote to individuals who have chosen to invest in this sort of stocks. However, these investors have an advantage in rights or claim to assets and profits of the company compared to the stockholders in the common stock category. They are allocated their dividends before any other group of shareholders and are given more priority than the common stockholders in a situation where the company becomes bankrupt. They have a supreme hold and right when it comes to the issuance of dividends. However, this particular set of people have limited powers when it comes to voting in a shareholders' meeting or in issues that may concern the welfare of the company. Their right to assets and profits of the company upon liquidation is second to the bondholders and higher than the common stockholders. However, a company is not regarded to be at default if it is unable to pay dividends to preferred stockholders as it is the case for bondholders. The purchase of preferred stock is usually made through the services of stockbrokers.

The significant difference between preferred and common shareholders is the mode of procedure that is adopted in the distribution of dividends in the case of a collapsed financial state or a company in distress. In the case of a liquidated company or a company in economic shambles, the preferred stockholders are paid the areas of their dividends before such payment can be made to the common stockholders.

Modes Of Attaining Profit In Stock

Stock investment has more investment risks than any other form of investment, hence, the necessity to familiarize you with the procedure and steps to ensure stock investment decisions and choices are carefully made to acquiring a suitable financial position, especially the status of financial freedom. After the entire process of investing, how then is money created? In what form is profit acquired from the money or time spent in the shares of a company? The earnings of shares invested by an investor are made though two primary forms; resale of stocks and dividends.

The resale of stocks: after a percentage of shares has been allocated to your name; for companies that do not pay dividends (dividends is the percentage of the earnings of your stocks that the management of the company chooses to pay to an investor.) It is not compulsorily held that you have ownership of that particular percentage of shares. If the company or business does not seem to appeal to you anymore, you could decide to sell your shares or stocks to another investor or an individual who has no connection or relation to the company in question. Therefore, the sale of stocks is a significant way to ensure that there is no loss of capital since you have the opportunity to sell your shares of a company in the case that you perceive a fluctuation in the finance or economy of the company.

The second reliable and significant form in which profit can be made is through dividends. Dividends refer to the payment or allowances received by shareholders based on their percentage of shares from the company or business they have a percentage of ownership. This should be regarded as regular payment of a shareholder or investor of any company, but this is not the case in every company. As an investor, you are not entitled to any percentage of dividends unless a cooperation decides to give it; therefore, not all businesses pay the profit on stocks. However, if you have invested in a company that does not pay dividends, you have the opportunity to reinvest your earnings if you do not intend to sell your shares. You can reinvest the profits acquired into the company that provided such an advantage in the first instance.

Therefore, the first option to make a profit from stock investment is much reliable as the individual controls the profit. In the case of dividends paid by companies or business, any management could decide at any point in time to put a stop to the payment of dividends if it does not suit their financial position at the time. Also, they can decide to increase or decrease the dividends paid; there is no fixed percentage of profits for companies that choose to pay.

Benefits of Attaining Stock Investments

Having explained the different steps and procedures that are put into a stock investment, you might still have concern or doubt of the benefits that this particular investment has to offer. However, investing in the stock market provides a variety of advantageous reasons and benefits. The following are some beneficial reasons for every individual to invest in the stock market:

- Diversification of funds: the stock markets provides a variety of categories or options for investors. Therefore, it allows the diversification of funds into different accounts or companies, allowing each individual to make different earnings based on the company and the percentage invested. Also, it helps to avoid total loss of funds, due to the diversification available in the general stock market, every individual is allowed to prevent a total loss of capital by investing in different accounts or companies that the stock market provides. Apart from the diversification of funds, it also offers the opportunity of diversification of assets. Some companies issue their investors or shareholders assets, identifying as an investor of such company would give you access to such assets and ensure that your assets are not based or focused on a particular subject matter and area.

- Easy access: A large number of individuals are more interested in ideas that can be easily accessed than those which prove difficult. The most accessible mode of access in this time is technology, stock markets and stocks can be approached and gotten through the internet, this is due to the technological innovations that have been put in place through the years. The access to stocks is readily made available with the intervention or help of the brokerage accounts or firms. The process needed is to identify a brokerage firm and input the information required from you. With details adequately attributed, you are ready to be a shareholder or investor of any company that needs your services.

- Option to invest in smaller accounts: some individuals are not interested in the investment of funds because they believe their funds would be at a loss. Stock market investing gives you the option to invest a small number of funds and not your total funds. This is done through the establishment of the Systematic Investment Plan (SIP).

- Inter-continental investment: it is essential to mention that stock investment is not restricted to a particular country. You are given the opportunity and option to invest in businesses and companies within and outside your country. The prospect of inter-continental investments is closely associated with the diversification benefit. Therefore, you make profits in funds or accounts that are different from the country inhabited by you. Also, it helps to attain assets in these countries.

- Partnership: in some situations, individuals are not allowed or permitted to participate in the task or jobs that they truly desire because of various reasons. The option of stock investing allows investing or partner with companies whose vision is closely related to yours. This may not be the case in some situations. In some cases, the partnership is needed because you do not have the right funds to establish a business idea.

- Attainment of dividends: for companies or businesses that issue profits to their investors, this is a standard benefit of stock investment. Majorly, it is you attaining more money from a company or business than what you invested; doubling your money or capital. Therefore, for an individual interested in passive income, the stock investment option is a pleasant way to earn while doing nothing, especially when you have a substantial percentage of funds.

Stock markets and investing is an essential aspect of financial freedom to be considered. It helps to grow not only an individual economy but also the national economy of the country or state an individual belongs. Therefore, with stock investing, you are enabled to increase with the growth of the nation's economy.

This is possible because as the economy of any society is strengthened, there is an increase in jobs provided and income; this allows the products of every company to get more audience. Therefore, the growth of the economy of a nation is vital to the growth of a company, as a result of this, paramount to your attainment of financial freedom.

CHAPTER SIX

Exchange-Traded Fund (ETF) Investing

For individuals who are interested in the profit of investment but the available options in stock investment does not favour or satisfy them. The topic of exchange-traded fund brings a change in your situation of finance as it offers investment in stock, bonds and other assets. Individuals interested that are interested in the provided investment options available would find the knowledge and understanding of exchange-traded fund needful. The establishment of the ETF plan is rooted in the Index Participation Shares of 1989 which had trade ties with the American Stock Exchange (ASE) and also, the Philadelphia Stock Exchange. These firms or institutions can be considered as the genesis of this particular investment option.

- Mutual Fund: this refers to a combination of funds or money collected from shareholders or investors to be invested in securities, these securities include stocks, bonds and some other assets. These funds or capital invested are usually monitored or managed by certified or qualified financial advisors, who ensure that the funds are appropriately managed and allocated to ensure profitable gain for the investors. Mutual funds are similar to exchange-traded funds because they both include a combination of assets and offers investors an opportunity to diversify.

- Underlying Asset or Index: an underlying asset is used to identify the main object that gives value, meaning or helps to identify the main subject of the contract.

What Is an Exchange Traded Fund (ETF)?

Having been familiarized with the history and establishment of the exchange-traded fund, the question "what is an ETF?" then arises. It is important to regard this particular question because it is the base which every other point or idea of ETF attains meaning and understanding for potential investors. To simplify the topic discussed in this chapter; it is crucial to define the term briefly- mutual funds, which would be referred to during your course of the exchange-traded fund. This term is subsequently discussed briefly;

Therefore, an exchange-traded fund (ETF) is a fund; as implied by the name. It allows its participants a variety of securities in trade in different investment options of exchange. The securities of the exchange-traded fund offer many investment options individually. However, these options are often combined in some cases, such as commodities, bonds and stocks. The principles of the exchange-traded fund may be compared to mutual funds because of the variety of investment options like stocks and bonds to be traded. It is also similar to an ordinary stock, in the case that it allows shares to be sold throughout the day, unlike the mutual funds which only trades once per day and this opportunity is only available after the market has closed. The exchange-traded funds have the attribute of fluctuation similar to ordinary stock; hence, the reason for the increase and decrease in prices of exchange-traded funds for both sellers and buyers.

The option or idea of exchange-traded funds is attractive primarily to individuals who are interested in diversification, both diversification of assets and funds. It does not offer a solid choice in assets, unlike stocks, the reason it may attract more investors than the regular stock.

Types Of Exchange Traded Fund

It is essential to attune or familiarize every individual or potential participant of the exchange-traded funds with the different types available, and to highlight the advantageous each option would provide. The various types of exchange-traded funds are used to generate profit and other beneficial provisions. The following are the types of exchange-traded funds:

- Bond Exchange Traded Fund: this refers to exchange-traded funds that invests in bonds. This particular kind is common in the fixed income category, mainly because the new and old prices are available to all shareholders or investors as they are traded on stock. However, this specific category of exchange-traded funds usually thrives when the economy is in a recession because money is often moved from stocks to bonds by investors. This is a significant indicator of the situation of an economy.

- Sector Exchange Traded Funds: it tracks a particular industry or market or sector rather than the whole or available general market. The sector exchange-traded funds invest in the assets or securities of a precisely defined sector. Take, for instance, the sector exchange-traded fund may only track the index for financial stocks, energy stocks or technology stocks; it depends solely on the area specified. It provides the option or opportunity to invest in a company without the stress of combining the individual stocks provided in that specific sector. This particular exchange-traded fund is commonly based on the United States-based stocks. This does not limit an individual who seeks to invest globally as some individuals are participants of this; the global investment option is explicitly done to gain from the sector's performance worldwide. However, in choosing to invest in a particular sector, it is important to identify or research if the sector is indeed a classification. This is the point of the establishment of the Global Industry Classification Standard (GICS). There are many sectors available in the world, and each sector has a sub-sector that is attributed. Hence, the role of the GICS in highlighting and defining the classification of sectors.

- Inverse/Short/Bear Exchange Traded Fund: this involves the use of various derivatives to gain from the loss or decline in the value of the underlying assets. The inverse exchange-traded funds entail holding minimal positions, and it also allows the opportunity of lending some securities and selling them; however, with the desire to repurchase them at a lower price.

- Commodity Exchange Traded Fund: this is an investment in physical or common commodities and natural resources. Usually, this type of ETF is focused on a particular kind of merchandise or on investments that would be made based on the conclusion of the contract. It is important to note that an individual who purchases a commodity exchange-traded fund has ownership rights to the set of deals that are backed up by a commodity, not a physical asset. The most recognized and popular products usually invested in are oil and gas, gold, silver. The investment in the gold commodity is so popular that it was among the first commodities invested; it was officially identified as an ETF commodity by Benchmark Asset Management Company Private Ltd in India in May 2002. Also, the popularity of the gold commodity can be attributed to the recognition of the SPDR Gold Shares as of the second-largest exchange-traded fund in November 2010. Unlike every other exchange-traded fund that has been discussed, this kind of exchange-traded fund does not track indexes because it does not invest in securities.

- Currency Exchange Traded Funds: these exchange-traded funds have the sole purpose of providing foreign currencies with investment options and exposure. This particular exchange-traded fund is the largest in the world due to the currency investment exposure option it offers.

Exchange Traded Funds Strategy

The exchange-traded funds are a suitable way to financial freedom, and it is also an ideal start for beginner investors because of the many benefits it provides, benefits such as cost-effectiveness, diversification and tax benefits. However, these exchange-traded funds can only be used to its full effectiveness with the understanding and strategic choices in the process. Therefore, it is of fundamental importance to familiarize you with the features that make ETF one of the most efficient strategies to attaining a financially free status. The following are some of the most critical features and plans that must be applied to make the most of the exchange-traded fund.

1. Fixed dollar amount: this involves the purchase of an asset in the amount of a specific fixed dollar, notwithstanding, the change that is attributed to the cost or price of such asset; it remains the fixed dollar amount. Majority of the percentage of investors are individuals who have a stable salary source and would be able to save or contribute some rate of their basic pay. If you are capable of doing this, then you should invest or contribute a portion of your basic pay to an exchange-traded fund or a group of them. This particular principle of contribution or investment would help to teach and establish the policy of saving, which is essential to the attainment of financial freedom. To become indeed financially free, you must have grown familiar with the

discipline of saving as it helps control expenses. Also, this helps to secure your funds and lower the risks on the money invested. The situation of a fixed amount accumulated a more significant percentage of interest or profit when the exchange-traded fund is law, and a lower percentage while high which helps to secure your finance in a financial state and sometimes above.

2. Allocation of assets: as the title illustrates, this involves the distribution of a portion of a whole to different categories of assets; stocks, bonds and commodities. This is most effective for individuals interested in the diversification advantage of exchange-traded funds. The exchange-traded fund has a low investment tolerance which allows participants to set an asset allocation strategy depending on their tolerance of risk and investment time.

3. Rotation of sectors: exchange-traded funds allows participants and investors to participate in different sectors depending on the current situation of the economy.

4. Invest in markets that provide ETFs: exchange-traded funds are available in the stock markets. There are exchange-transfer funds for different sectors. Therefore, you only have to identify the ETF specifies in your particular area of interest.

5. Identify a sector of investment: after the interest to be part of the exchange-traded fund has been recognized. The most important thing is to identify the area you would like to invest as the exchange-traded fund offers investment options to individuals who show interest.

Benefits of Exchange Traded Funds

Over time, many individuals have identified as participants of the mutual funds due to the securities provided. However, the establishment of the exchange-traded fund offers a different approach to the benefits that were only peculiar to mutual funds. Therefore, it is essential to be aware of the advantages of every investment option to ensure that your interest in a particular field or sector of investment does not collapse. It is for this reason that some of the advantages of the exchange-traded funds over other investment options are being discussed.

- Availability of diversification: an investor in finance may have an interest in the discussions or profits provided by different other sectors but might be limited because of inexperience or ineffectiveness in such an area. However, this does not seem to be a significant issue with the provisions of ETF, which allows an investor to gain exposure in a specific sector. The exchange-traded fund is now available under every recognized sector or aspect in the world. Exchange-transfer funds are traded in assets, commodity and class. Through the purchase of one particular fund, the exchange-traded fund can help to identify other securities, such as stocks and bonds. It also helps to reduce the risk of loss due to the spread of funds or capital across various markets and assets, as a result of this, offering a more significant income rate than the regular investment options. The most common example of this diversification option available being put to good use and portraying effectiveness is the Vanguard Stock Market Exchange, Traded Fund. They are participants in investing over three thousand five hundred (3,500) United States stocks. The feature of diversification is evident as their investment involves companies in various, if not all the sectors that are tied to the economy of the United States.

- Cost-effective: in stock investing and mutual funds, active management requires the payment of funds and other expenses which vary depending on requirement demanded by the level of management. The costs that may be incurred through the process of management may include administrative expenses, marketing costs and distribution costs. However, the exchange-traded funds are of low cost compared to the mutual funds, and they are recognized for this particular feature. They are identified and known for the low expense ratio that it offers investors, and this specific ratio is usually within the range of 0.10% and 0.25%. The exchange-traded funds do not require any actual work or participation, hence the reason for the drastic difference between it and the managed mutual funds. It usually does not require significant management, and it is even regarded as a passively- managed fund because it does not require research or analysis.

Also, the exchange-traded funds are low in cost in the aspect of notifications, statements and transfers that are required, unlike the traditional funds which give investors the right or entitlement to get notifications and reports regularly. In ETFs, sponsors are expected only to provide the information to direct participants and capital owners of specific creation units.

Lastly, another cost-effective feature of the exchange-traded fund is that it does not require redemption fees like mutual funds. The investors or shareholders that are participants of the exchange-traded fund can avoid the short-term fees of redemption needed by the mutual funds.

- Tax benefits: comparing the structure of the mutual funds and the exchange-traded funds, the former incurs a higher capital profit taxes than the former. In the case that the exchange-traded fund would even incur tax on the capital gains, it is only taxed at the time or moment the exchange-traded the investor sells the fund. In this same subject, the mutual funds are taxed on capital gains throughout the investment time rather than the time sold. However, in considering the payment of dividends, the payment of dividends to the exchange-traded fund investors is less advantageous compared to the traditional mutual funds. The exchange transfer funds issues two significant categories of dividends (profits of a particular investment), which are qualified and unqualified dividends. Each of these categories has a set requirement that confirms it to be a qualified or unqualified dividend. An exchange-traded fund is approved to attain qualified dividends when the particular exchange-traded a recognized or specific investor has owned fund for at least sixty (60) days before the fixed or expected date for dividends to be paid out. The qualified dividends offer tax rate depends on the rate of income by the investor or shareholder. However, the rate available is between the range 5% to 15% while unqualified dividends are taxed based on the investor's profit tax rate. However, the income of investment (dividends) gotten from companies in the exchange-traded fund is reinvested immediately, unlike the mutual funds whose reinvestment time may vary.

- Flexibility in Trade: The ordinary trade in a mutual fund is allowed only once during the day, this time is secluded to the end of the market when the market closes. Investors are required to wait until the Net Asset Value (NAV) is asserted for them to know the price of the new shares and the profit made from the shares sold. This does not seem to be an obstacle for some people, although it can be obstructive for individuals who belong to the category of short-term investors and those who require flexibility in their finances. However, the exchange-traded funds shares the similarity of stock investments which allows investors or shareholders to buy and sell shares or assets during the day, and the exchange-traded funds also permit this.

This allows investors to place specific orders in place to avoid certain risks or loss. An example of such a request is a stop-loss order, and this particular market order allows investors to sell some of their assets or sell out entirely of the exchange-traded fund, at a specific price. The flexibility of the exchange-traded funds also allows investors the benefit of placing orders in different ways.

- Niche Trading: This particular benefit is most identifiable with the sector exchange-traded fund. The exchange-traded fund allows investors or individuals to invest in some areas that the regular mutual funds do not provide. Due to the classification of the GCIS, exchange-traded funds may cover more than the ordinary sectors, and it encompasses the sub-sectors also.

CHAPTER SEVEN

Options Trading, Rental Properties, and Flipping Houses

The previous chapters have explored various options that could aid or increase the possibility of financial freedom for each individual. There are three basic options or categories of tasks or opportunities that do not require the investment of capital in a company or business by buying stocks or shares. The options that would be discussed in the course of this chapter also do not require you to be a retailer or an employee, and these options offer participants or individuals the opportunity to be identified with the "self-made" financially free status. The possibilities that belong to this category are options trading, rental property, and flipping houses. The effects of these financial income decisions on a current economic state would be discussed; also, the effectiveness of these options will be one of the subject issues in this particular section of the book. These options (options trading, rental property, and flipping houses) are categorized in the same chapter because they have similar requirements. They can be referred to as sub-sectors under the general sector of finance, basic pay, or salary received from the issuance of passive income (salary received from tasks that do not demand extensive activities from an individual. This brings us to the junction where it is vital to understand the meaning and content of these options.

An Introduction to Options Trading

As the name or title of this particular option implies, this is a trade. Therefore, options refer to a contract or agreement that allows individuals to trade for a specific subject of interest or any underlying asset. The business in options is not a compulsion for investors. However, it is allowed for any investor who presents or showcases interest in the sale or purchase of securities, exchange-traded funds, and also underlying assets. An option is a recognized or qualified agreement that allows an investor to buy and sell underlying assets or securities within a specific time range within a particular time. The purchase, that is, the buying and selling of options which include underlying assets and securities, can be done through the normal process of purchasing various other assets or stocks. Therefore, options are purchased through the services of a broker when an individual has created or activated a brokerage account. Although it might be presented or understood that options are overly efficient, they are not void of the risks present in other investment options. Therefore, an investor that is in the business or interest of options trading has to be aware of the risks that are present in this particular trade. This is the primary reason for the warning that every brokerage service offers participants before the contract is fully enforced. This warning usually includes the fact that options trading consists of a significant risk of losing profits. Two major terms are significant in the purchase and engagement of options trading, and these are "call option" and "put option." The call option refers to the situation where an individual or investor buys a particular percentage of options that allow him to purchase shares at a different time, while the put option will enable you to buy an option that allows you to sell shares at a later or different time. Furthermore, in considering the role of options trading and comparing it to stock investment, this particular option does not equal the entitlement or right to claim ownership of a specific company. However, options to a significant extent is considered at a more substantial advantage because it puts participants at lower risk by giving them the right or entitlement to withdraw or rescind an options contract at any time it seems favorable.

In finance and investment generally, these options are commonly referred to by most businesses or companies and even individuals as derivatives because they are a sub-sector of securities. They are called derivatives because their price or cost is dependent on the price of something else. That is, the value of a derivative or options, in this case, is derived from the cost of a different product. Therefore, in the modern-day, many products are derivatives of other things. Take, for instance; the paper is a derivative of wood, coffee is a derivative of cocoa, and also a stock option is derived from a stock. Therefore, the price of options is derived from the value that is attached to a different asset.

There are two basic types of options, and these are the American options and European Options. The names do not imply that these options are different based on the geographical location; the only difference is the terms of period or time of exercise. The American options refer to options that are exercised at any time within the date of expiration and purchase, while the European options can only be applied on the date it expires.

Advantages of Options Trading

After the definition and explanation of the options, it is essential to clearly state the benefits that are available to individuals who plan to participate in this particular category. Therefore, the reasons for every individual to use options trading is discussed in subsequent paragraphs. These reasons are also the essential benefits that are feasible for the participants or investors of options trading.

- The benefit of speculation: this is a chance or a review on the wager of the price of assets and the position it would take later, that is, the possibility that it could increase or reduce. Individuals who are effective in the use of this particular advantage are referred to as speculators. Therefore, based on the analysis made by a speculator, he might believe that the price attached to a specific stock might increase, based on this thought, the speculator might purchase a stock or put the call option in place to purchase the stock. Therefore, the purchase of a call option protects individuals from risks and provides an acceptable level of leverage than buying the stock itself without the certainty that the price would be increase or decrease.

- The benefit of a hedge: hedging refers to something that provides security from risks or losses. The basic function of options recognized by individuals is its hedging function.

Therefore, under options, investments have the opportunity to be insured by their investors. You are given a similar benefit or relief that is available to your other belongings, this benefit is an insurance policy which helps to ensure that your investments are covered by insurance in the case of liquidation.

An Introduction to Rental Property

Most individuals have friends or family members that are tenants or inhabitants of a home that does not legitimately belong to them. However, these people are not the subject of discussion in this section. Instead, this section is dedicated to the actual owners of the houses or individuals interested in this particular trade.

Rental property refers to properties that are purchased by an individual who is usually referred to as an investor. Other individuals or tenants usually rent this purchased property or home, this agreement or relationship between these individuals is contained in a contract known as a rental agreement or a lease. Most of these rental properties are invested in with the primary intention of profiting when leased or through the resale of the property at a later time. In a few situations, it is done to earn through both of the stated options. In a rental property, there is a significant requirement to qualify as a property investor, and a property investor could refer to a single individual or a group of people. A registered company or business could also decide to invest in rental property. However, there are two primary classifications of rental properties; these are the residential rental property and thee commercial rental property.

The residential rental property refers to a category or group of homes that are restricted to be inhabited by individuals a living and dwelling space. This particular category consists of various structures of homes, and it includes apartment units and duplexes and bungalows as long as it is beneficial for the individual dwelling in such space. This particular investment is quite attractive and attainable by most investors because every individual can relate on this level due to their prior experience as tenants. Also, this particular section of investment is capable of offering a stable income source monthly or annually, and its tax advantages are more attractive than other investment options.

The commercial rental property refers to the category of properties that are used solely for business and commercial activities. It encompasses both buildings and land that provide profit for a particular institution. However, if a building is registered as a commercial rental property, it has different laws that apply to it, and the percentage and process of taxation are different compared to the residential rental property.

Steps to Ensuring a Profitable Investment In Rental Property

Having defined the term "rental property," it is important to elaborate on the essential measures that would ensure investing in rental property is profitable to you as it has been for other individuals.

- Identification: it is vital to identify and understand the principle of rental property. The sector of rental property or real estate investment has helped to establish some of the wealthiest people in the world. As this is one of your many goals, to reach financial freedom, it is no surprise that you would seek the benefits of this principle to identify with the same economic status. However, this might be a beneficial investment decision for them, but it is not always the case for every individual. The position of a property owner is infused with a lot of responsibilities and quite demanding. Therefore, you must believe that you can deliver on all grounds that pertain to your duties as a property owner.

- Acquisition of skills: most new or developing property owners do not have the funds to hire a maintenance specialist after the investment of money into the rental property. Hence, the need for them to acquire some primary skills to attend to damages that might occur in the house. However, this does not signify that they would be in charge of repairs for a long time, this might only be needed until the profits of their investments, that is, the payment of rent by the tenants is acquired. In the case that the property owner decides to remain the handyman for such an apartment or building, he saves the cash or funds that would have been required for professional workmanship.

- Settle debts: this particular requirement has been emphasized throughout this book. For any investment option to yield profits for investors, such an investor is required to have paid debt, or else the interest of such debt would continue to affect his savings. However, in real estate or rental property, it is not necessary to pay the debt before embarking on your real estate quest if the rental property would provide profit that is higher than the debt. Even in this situation, ensure that your income or amount of salary is higher than the mortgage.

- Avoid flipping: as a beginner in the business of rental property, it is very attractive to bargain a fixer-upper to renovate and turn into a rental property. There are several detriments to your finance when you choose a fixer-upper to be flipped. Such houses are expensive to renovate, although, at the time bought, you might be of the opinion that you are saving a large percentage of money. While in reality, you would spend more than the original budget if you had purchased a house that does not need to be flipped.

Therefore, it is more reasonable to buy a house that needs minor or no repairs at all. This particular opinion is upheld by Matt Holmes, Chief Executive Officer of Holmes Real Estate Group.

- Calculate your profits: although a lot of individuals are familiar with the popular term, "do not count your hens before they hatch." In this particular case, the determination of profit is important as it keeps you in tune with the primary goal or reason for the rental property. This specific idea also helps to keep track of your profits and expenses; this also helps to determine if the rental property provides a valuable return compared to other investment options. Cash-on-cash performance in stocks offers as high as 7.5% in profit in some situations while the bonds offer 4.5% in some cases. However, the rental property may offer a 6% gain in some circumstances, compared to the other investment options, the percentage of profit from this particular option is favorable. Also, there is a probability that this profit could increase over time.

- Location: it is essential to get a low-cost home of the right location as this would determine the level of availability of tenants. Therefore, the percentage of expenses obtained from a particular home is based on the total amount of the house when purchased. In choosing the location of a rental property, some key features are to be considered; these features are the tax rate of the properties, low crime rate, a reasonable school area.

How Effective is Rental Property to Attaining Freedom?

Rental property is an option of passive income, and it is even one of the primary ways of attaining passive income. Therefore, the ownership of a real estate or rental property alongside a regular job or no job at all is a definite way to attaining a financially free status. This is a primary option of investing to attain financial freedom, especially for individuals or investors who are averse to stock market investments. The rental property provides the opportunity to earn passive income, for property owners who do not intend to fix damages in the house themselves, this is a suitable suggestion for passive income. The process of becoming the owner of a rental property does not require any active participation or management, apart from the initial capital invested in the purchase and general upkeep cost. Therefore, you can be interested and invest in a rental property without it damaging your daily job, routine, or schedule.

There is an enormous growth in income available to real estate owners. As a property owner, after the investment of funds to earn such title, there is a growth in the percentage of income. The profit or revenue gotten from the real estate or rental property does not remain static; it is so beneficial that the benefit of your investment grows with an increase in real estate value. Also, comparing the stability in the amount of both the stock market and rental properties, the latter is more stable in value, providing a hedge compared to stock investing.

The other investment options provide the opportunity to invest in assets such as stock and shares, and these are all assets that may not be visible; that is, they are not physical. However, the option of investing in rental property is a tangible and more dependable asset because it is something you can monitor closely compared to stocks and shares.

Conclusively, in the course of investing in rental property, it is essential to have realistic and reasonable expectations concerning profits. It is important to note that although rental property would provide a large salary or paycheck at some point, this is not done from the beginning stage, and it may take a little more than the expected duration in a situation where the wrong property was selected. Therefore, the choice of property is a critical factor to be considered in rental property investments. Also, an individual with little or no experience in the field could partner with a corporation to have a professional understanding of the workings of rental properties.

An Introduction to Flipping Houses

Through the course of initiating you with the concept, idea, or principle of rental houses, the term "flipping" or "flipping houses" was mentioned a couple of times. Hence, the necessity to initiate you with this particular option in this section.

"Flipping" as a general term is the purchase of an asset or assets to be sold for profit rather than withholding the position or status of ownership. This term is usually affiliated with real estate or houses, and this is the focal point of the discussion in this section; the flipping of houses and not flipping as a general idea.

Therefore, flipping in this context usually refers to the purchase of a house or real estate property and selling it within the time frame of a year for a quick profit. In some cases, it refers to refurbishing or repairing the house before it is put up for sale. This is a common source of income for people, especially in the United States, where it was reported that 207,088 houses were flipped in the year 2017. There are two significant types of flipping. Firstly, there is one where investors buy properties that are in a primarily appreciating market, and these identified houses are immediately resold without the investors rehabbing the physical condition of the property. This procedure or particular type is carried out based on the status of the market and not the terms of property. The second type is referred to as the reno flip. The reno flip constitutes the renovation of the targeted property to be flipped, these renovations or fixings are done based on the knowledge of the investor on what potential buyers would like to improve. The idea of flipping is so lucrative that it provides the option or opportunity of wholesale. In the business of wholesaling of houses or properties, an individual who has been recognized or noticed to be exceptionally productive in identifying undervalued houses establishes an agreement or a contract to purchase a particular property. However, the purchase of such property is subject to a period of inspection, after the concluded period, the wholesale contractor is allowed to sell the rights of the approved property to an investor who pays him a percentage. The property sold by the wholesale investor does not necessarily have to be flipped by the buyer; he is allowed to settle for the property as home after renovations and repairs.

The business or idea of real estate also consists of some risks that can be detrimental to the financial state of the individual. For instance, if an investor has decided to invest in a recognized zone, such an individual cannot identify the time the value of such a market could decrease. Therefore, the value attached to an exchange could fall at any time; the investor is disadvantaged as the assets would continue to depreciation, which is a loss for him.

How to Flip Houses Efficiently?

A lot of individuals might be interested in flipping houses, and many more might have experienced this line of income. They might even believe that flipping houses are not a reasonable or reliable investment option because of the risks that are present in this particular field. However, this does not have to be the case for every individual, because, with the basic knowledge of flipping houses, profit can be efficiently made. Therefore, this section will consist of the requirements of house flipping and the necessary steps to ensure maximum effectiveness in the flipping of houses.

Ensure that you have enough capital or credit. The option of house flipping can not be useful for you if you do not have a substantial percentage of money as capital or excellent credit. These are basic requirements in the renovation and purchase of the property or house that would be eventually flipped. Therefore, it essential to have an excellent credit score. If this is not the case, then you should endeavor to create one now. The credit score is vital as it determines the interest that would be gotten or given on a home loan once flipping starts. Flipping of houses requires plenty of cash as a significant amount of money is needed to purchase the property and to carry out necessary renovations.

To What Extent is Flipping Houses A Success?

In ensuring that flipping houses do not become detrimental to an individual's finance, it is important to understand the following steps before the flipping of houses.

- Understand the targeted market: before you purchase a property to be flipped, you need to know the interest of the targeted people at that particular period. In house flipping, to ensure that profit is made, an individual can not make speculation on the desire of targets.

- Identify the available financial options: there are various financing options available in real estate property projects. Ensure that you consider each one to choose a specific one that assists your particular situation. This specific idea would help you in making the right decisions for your homes.

- Analysis: ensure that the expenses and profit that can be made from a particular project is appropriately analyzed. The 70% rule is the basic guideline adopted by most flippers, and this is used in their analysis before a house is purchased. The 70% rule provides that investors should not pay higher than 70% of the ARV (After Repair Value.)

- Negotiation: this is a crucial requirement in house flipping as it determines the percentage of expenses in a particular deal or on a specific property. Therefore, negotiation in renovations or repairs would help save a tremendous amount of money.

- Knowledge of average projects: agreed, not every property or house would require the same renovation, however, the experience of what an average repair on a regular day would help determine if a particular property is a good deal, especially for individuals who plan to renovate.

- Networking: it is important to network with potential buyers. The act of networking does not require a house that needs to be flipped; you can talk and discuss with them to understand the renovations and kind of houses that would interest them. Also, it saves you the need or stress to search for buyers when a property is ready to be flipped, and it gives you profit when the market is still of high value.

- Offer: once an investor has identified a potential property that would be of profit to him, it is necessary to make an offer to purchase. However, before the offer is presented, ensure that you have recognized the highest amount you can pay for such property without affecting your profit.

- Contracting: some individuals might not be interested in the contracting business because they believe that they can handle the repairs themselves. This is a fair opinion;

however, you need to be able to distinguish between repairs that can be handled by you and those that need professional attention.

- Resell or re-list: in flipping houses, there are two available options, you can choose to sell your house by yourself, or you could list it to a realtor who lists the house to be sold in the Multiple Listing Service database. Although many individuals may not show interest in the services of a realtor due to costs attached to services. As a beginner, it is advisable to employ their services irrespective of the fees because the resale of a property by yourself might take time, and there is a probability the property might have reduced in value if it is eventually sold.

To ensure that flipping houses is a success, the above procedures or steps should be strictly adhered to as they are the determinants of the success of this trade or investment option.

CHAPTER EIGHT

Retire Early

Retirement in plain terms refers to an end or the withdrawal from an individual's daily occupation or life, and it also signifies the close on an active job or working lifestyle. Closely related to this term is the position of a semi-retirement. Semi-retirement refers to a reduction in the working hours of an individual. Most individuals who choose to retire before the suggested time of retirement do so because of their eligibility status for pensions. However, some individuals retire because of unfavorable situations. Situations like illnesses or incapacity to function efficiently in a particular position might demand retirement in some cases.

It should be noted that retirement has not always been a principle that existed in most countries or institutions due to the life expectancy rate and the absence of retirement plans, this directly meant that employed individuals had to work till death. However, in the later 19th century and early 20th century, the concept of retirement was established. This principle was first introduced in Germany in 1889. The historical antecedence of retirement is not the focal topic of this chapter; this section is expected to specialize in the role of early retirement and financial freedom.

However, the option of early retirement in attaining financial freedom might seem ironical as it is a means to generate funds and income through the basic pay. However, this position can assist in achieving financial freedom and has gained recognition over the years. This principle or terminology is commonly referred to as the FIRE, that is, the Financial Independence and Retire Early movement. An individual is considered to have retired early if withdrawal from a job or current occupation is made before the tenure approved by the government or law that concerns such a corporation. Not every individual that claims to have retired early has applied for it, some individuals in such a situation because their employment contract was terminated before the usual time. Still, they would instead employ the euphemistic term of early retirement.

What Is The FIRE Movement?

Financial Independence and Retire Early (FIRE) movement was established based on the content of the 1992 book by Vicki Robin and Joe Dominguez, titled "Your Money or Your Life." involves the attainment of financial freedom and independence through early retirement. The main principle or idea in the book that launched the FIRE movement is the belief that individuals usually trade their life energy for money through their dedication to their jobs or their involvement in the workforce. It is a retirement movement that allows participants or individuals to retire earlier than the expected traditional time or plan. However, for the provision of financial independence and retire early movement to work for you, potential participants should have begun contributing at least 70% of their salary or basic pay to a retirement savings plan, plans like the 401(k)s and the thrift savings plan. Individuals who adhere strictly to the guidance of the FIRE movement might eventually be allowed to quit their jobs and survive on the contributions made to their retirement savings. However, the withdrawal from the retirement savings has to be done minimally to ensure an individual does not exhaust the entirety of the savings. The contents and movement of financial independence and early retirement is usually adopted by individuals whose lifestyles consist of extreme or maximum saving of their salary, and these individuals ensure to save up to 70% of their income during their years of working with a traditional corporation. However, once they have attained a reasonable goal, in some situations, 1 million, they quit their current job or occupation, some even go as far as quitting the traditional workforce. These people survive on the discipline of spending their savings wisely and not elaborately; the main participants of this movement make small withdrawals from their savings through the years. This usually falls between withdrawing 3% to 4% of the savings annually. However, this range of withdrawal is not a compulsion for every individual, as the percentage of annual or yearly withdrawals would be determined by the total amount available in such an account. The survival of the FIRE movement depends on the withdrawal percentage, diligence in monitoring expenses, extreme maintenance of the available funds and reallocation of investments by each individual. However, this plan also provides its risks, the failure or decrease in the value of the stock market or the interest rate might lead to a defect or failure of the financial independence and early retirement plan. However, the FIRE movement has a variety of types to fit specific situations of each individual, and these variations provide a guideline for devotees of each to live by, this assists the success of the movement in individual lifestyles. These variations are subsequently discussed:

- Fat Financial Independence, Retire Early: this category refers to an individual who has more advantage than the traditional retirement investor, that is, their savings percentage might be higher than the regular savings. Individuals who belong to this category have a normal lifestyle and are individuals who save a percentage higher than that which is expected from an ordinary retirement investor. These people spend more money on ensuring they have their chosen lifestyle compared to other variants, and their expenses are usually between a million dollars and more.

- Lean Financial Independence, Retire Early: individuals in this category save to the extremes. Their savings usually affects or dictates their lifestyle. It is the strict adherence to substantial investment savings for retirement and a minimal lifestyle. This particular category refers to people whose lifestyle are based or controlled with less than $25,000 (twenty-five thousand dollars) per year.

- Barista Financial Independence, Retire Early: some individuals have quit their regular day to day jobs. However, they still have income from being an employee of some sort. This category of people is explicitly categorized under the barista variation. This variation refers to individuals who have quit the regular jobs that pay them their normal salary but are still employees of minimal jobs which pay them to cover their current expenses. This is usually done to ensure their retirement savings funds is not squandered and are kept until they are compulsorily needed.

- Coast/Side Financial Independence, Retire Early: this particular variable is closely related to the barista. Precisely like the barista FIRE, these individuals have quit their jobs and are employees of a part-time job to cover their current expenses. However, the variation between these two is that the coast FIRE proponents can afford their current daily costs with their retirement funds without an adverse effect on their retirement savings.

Steps to an Effective FIRE Plan

Financial independence and early retirement is more than quitting a job or writing a retirement plan. The idea or principle might seem simple in theory, but the execution? Not so simple, there are some specific guidelines and options that must be considered, confirmed and put in motion determine if an individual is ready to be a participant of the financial independence and early retirement movement. Hence, the need to highlight some of the basic requirements and steps of the FIRE movement.

- Step 1: identify the kind of lifestyle that would benefit you. The first step to ensuring that the FIRE movement is effective for you is to identify the type of lifestyle that resonates with your personality. The biggest problem that is faced in many financial decisions and institution is the fact that individuals show interest-based on the profit or money offered by such a decision. Based on the opinions from the book "Your Money or Your Life," individuals are made aware that you can always make money through whatever means you decide, however, the time of your life that is lost can never be retrieved. Therefore, before you consider the monetary benefits of a decision, consider the effect it would have on your lifestyle. If you have decided on the kind of lifestyle you want, then you can determine whether the principle of FIRE would work for you, and also determine the percentage of money that would be reasonable for you to save.

- Step 2: calculate your expenses and budget. Every financial journey decision demands a correctly laid down budget. Therefore, after the proper identification of the kind of lifestyle that would benefit you, it is essential to make a budget for the cost of sustenance. Thus, the process of calculating your dream lifestyle would define and highlight the percentage of money that needs to be saved annually; supposedly you have a specific age you would like to retire. Also, in calculating money, it is not only the cost of lifestyle that should be considered. The tax that would be demanded on such savings should also be considered, the allowances of inflation or deflation in whatever market should also be considered in whatever calculation made.

- Step 3: Prioritize. After, the budget or the rate of money that should be saved annually has been decided. It is essential to prioritize your expenses to ensure that you are living comfortably and wisely. Therefore, an individual interested in the provisions of FIRE should be interested in spending on necessities and valuable things rather than items that are desired, wanted but not needed. Therefore, all the extra money that could have been spent on desires can be committed or contributed to a savings account because, in most situations, the height of your savings rate would determine the suitable time of retirement. The height of your savings rate is dependent on consistent contribution, to ensure that saving does not become a burden or chore to you, ensure that you view it as a means to live the lifestyle you desire. Savings is simply a means to a goal. The only procedure that would determine your participation in the Financial Independence and Retire Early movement is saving and investing in a retirement savings plan. To fast track your journey to financial freedom, it is vital to create a balance between the basic pay or salary, the money spent, and that which is contributed to your retirement savings. Conclusively, saving faster or quick attainment of financial independence demands a reduction in expenses which would lead to an increase in contributions.

- Step 4: Pay off your debts (good debts and bad debts). Surprisingly, debt is being referred to in the positive here as the only type of debt we are familiar with is the negative one. The concept of the good debt relates to debts that you can use to generate profit, and an example is the mortgage debt which is used for real estate investments and student loans when it helps to get a highly profitable job. However, the bad debt, as you may have guessed is the debt that is detrimental to your finances. Money is lost when it comes to bad debt. A generally or commonly known example of the bad debt is the credit card debt with an interest rate of up to

20%. In the case of FIRE, it is essential to pay up all existing debt as it is a loss of money on your terms. However, if you are an individual that has both the good and bad debt, the advisable strategy in paying them off is one that demands you to pay the debt with the highest interest rate, which in most cases is the credit card debt. This procedure of payment can be made based on the hierarchical order of interest rates.

- Step5: Participate in your current job to get a promotion and skills acquisition. Most of the money that would be contributed to your retirement savings plan would be procured from your full-time or regular job, hence, the need to ensure that you function to your fullest capacity to earn a raise. However, in most situations, specific individuals deserve a raise or a promotion, but they have been denied this advantage. It is necessary to demand a promotion if you belong to this category because the increase in salary or basic pay would increase the percentage of funds contributed to retirement savings, thereby causing a reduction in the number of years an individual has to endure before retirement.

- Step 6: Passive income. If you are unfamiliar with this term or unaware of it, this refers to side hustles or a regular job that allows you to earn without an active role. This is where the acquisition of skills in the previous step comes to play, and skill could hasten the amount of money contributed to your plan. However, your passive income does not necessarily have to be a skill. In this case, it is merely something you can do to acquire funds or money apart from your regular or full-time job; although the best passive income options are those jobs that determine or demands you to participate in activities that you generally enjoy.

- Step 7: Invest. Investment is fundamental in the Financial Independence and Retire Early plan. Investment has been discussed in various sections of this book and investing is not limited to only stocks. What does the investment option have to do with FIRE? If you intend to retire early, but all your funds and salary are locked up in a savings account without gaining profit from it, it could be a bit tiresome before an individual attains financial independence. However, when an individual can invest savings into an investment account, it fast tracks the entire saving process as the profit of investment or dividends can be reinvested and later moved to the retirement savings account when profit has been made from the initial capital. This is an essential procedure in attaining financial freedom with the early retirement plan. Basically, you are making a profit from your initial money, and both the profit made and the capital invested can be later contributed to the account. However, it is advisable to invest in the most dependable assets which are stocks, bonds and real estate. There are other available investment options, but these are the most dependable and effective ones. Also, it is necessary to ensure that a company, business or corporation is willing to pay dividends or profit of investment before the entire investment procedure is carried out. Therefore, an individual interested in investing in a company's stock is expected to have read or familiarized himself with the company's stock quote.

- Step 8: Build daily habits. Having followed the required steps to attaining financial independence as well as early retirement, you have to build habits of consistency in savings and persistence in sticking to the budget of expenses. Therefore, you have to consistently stick to the steps to have a beneficial effect of the FIRE plan. You cannot follow the steps religiously for a few months and abandon it at some point because you believe your financial state is doing well. Strict adherence would enable you the ease to adjust to the change in any case or situation.

Sustaining Financial Freedom/Independence After Retirement

The steps and ideas that are expected to be followed to ensure that every individual is allowed to be financially free are available to every individual. The steps to the attainment of early retirement as well as financial freedom have been stated. However, there is still an issue for individuals when it comes to the sustenance and management of money after retirement. As many individuals believe that it is quite impossible because the main reason to have a job is to make money and attain freedom. Even assuming that you have a secure retirement plan, there are unplanned expenses that could arise, and what way do you plan to reinstate the funds that have been unceremoniously withdrawn? These are questions that have been laid down and designed to be answered in this section of the chapter. The inability to settle these questions would discourage individuals from the objectives of this chapter; hence, the primary reason this issue is being discussed. Some of the ways to sustain financial freedom or independence after retirement are, through investments, budgeting, proper maintenance, a financial advisor, etc.

At the point of retirement is essential to set new life goals. Retirement signifies a new stage in life, and it is essential to set the expectations that would define this particular cycle of life to ensure that your current financial situation is not affected adversely by it. Therefore, it is important to set out or write out the current amount that you have in your savings account, and the percentage of daily expenses that your new lifestyle would require.

It is important to make a budget after the life goals or expectations have been clearly stated out. Therefore, it is advisable to make a budget for every sphere of your new lifestyle as this is the only way to ensure that your expenses are on track and your savings are not overspent to a position that would render you uncomfortable. The budget would create an awareness of the funds that are available and will discourage any attempt to overspend on wants rather than necessities.

Ensure that you do not create any debts. At this point, loans should not even be an option for you as it would only eat into your savings. Therefore, it is important to ensure that all high-interest loans like credit cards are paid in full balance each point. This particular option was previously emphasized because of the high-interest rate credit cards embody.

Indulge the available various investment opportunities. Some individuals might have a large retirement savings plan that they begin to squander the money or funds, simply because they claim not to have expenses. Instead of this, such individuals could invest funds in a company, business, corporation to receive the profit of their investment, thereby creating a mode of income for themselves and doubling their savings.

Also, it would be beneficial to employ the services of a financial advisor if the entire process of retirement math plan does not appeal to you. In most cases, it is helpful for individuals to seek professional help in allocating funds to each section of their lifestyle. This allocation is to ensure that they do not go over budget or budget less and have to remove emergency funds which would destroy the main point of creating a budget.

Benefits of Early Retirement

What do you have to gain after retirement? As a young person, why would I want to retire early when there are more experiences and benefits for me in the workforce. Firstly, you cannot know how advantages and essential an opportunity or something is to you until you give it a try, and often it is better to understand the advantages of a particular decision in discussions with people who have experienced such situation. Therefore, in determining if early retirement would be beneficial to you, it is advisable to seek the opinion of those who have succeeded in the quest. The quest, in this case, being early retirement.

- Early retirement and financial independence would make it easier to explore the world. Many individuals are interested in viewing more than the state, country or continent they are born. However, most people are unable to do this with complaints of time and funds. The FIRE plan is a significant way to live this lifestyle. However, some individuals might insist that this particular "benefit" is a disadvantage to their savings, they are not wrong about this, but there is a way to make this work. This can be done by balancing expensive countries or places with the inexpensive ones, and this technique has been tested by its proponents who had travelled the world for four years with the total cost of $30,879. The individuals with this testimony are Kristy Shen and Bryce Leung. They claim to spend less now that they are travelling the world compared to the expenses they had living in a major city.

- Early retirement would put you in a situation where you would not have to worry about money. For some individuals, their biggest challenge is the thought of their salary as they are living on paycheck to paycheck, however, individuals who have been able to sustain and adhere to a retirement plan can forfeit this concern. With strict adherence to a maintenance plan, their retirement savings might be enough to last them a lifetime

In conclusion, to ensure that you are contributing the most to your attainment of the financial independence and retirement plan, it is vital to have a consistent savings plan. The 401(k)s and the Thrift Savings Plan (TSP) are some ways to ensure consistency in retirement savings as they both offer automatic saving contributions which involve the withdrawal of a particular percentage from your account to your personal savings account. It also helps to receive contributions from the institution or corporation that might have employed you.

CONCLUSION

This entire book is sectioned in a way that each chapter gives a fresh and new option to the attainment of financial freedom. It helps that every chapter provides a new investment option or financial plan for individuals, therefore, it gives individuals a new idea of financial freedom. The fact that these investment plans and subjects have been suggested creates a state of realism that financial freedom or independence is a reasonable approach. The role of financial freedom for each individual is dependent on the strategy and decisions of each individual. The effectiveness of financial freedom or each of the options can not be generalized, although an estimate for the extent of effectiveness can be made.

However, many people desire the benefits of attaining the financially independence status but the truth in most situations is that they are not ready to sacrifice and dedicate the diligence and discipline required by financial freedom. Therefore, they find themselves in a situation where they have been able to adhere to the guidelines of financial freedom but once they perceive a small amount of independence in their finances, they abandon the laid down regimen that has gotten them to that particular stage. This is the primary reason for the majority of losses gotten by individuals in their quest to attaining financial freedom. This is not usually the fault of some individuals as some blogs or websites provide a ridiculous principle of living before the attainment of financial freedom. Imagine being advised that the attainment of financial freedom and independence would require you to sell all your materials and move into a trailer with your family of five or you would not buy good food, instead you should depend on food from dumpsters or waste from restaurants. These principles are impossible for anyone to adhere to and it defeats the whole purpose of attainment of financial freedom. Individuals are not expected to starve and live unhealthily because they want an independent status, you are expected to live your specifically chosen lifestyle before and during your course to attaining a financially free status.

Individuals should be familiarized with the ideology that the attainment of financial freedom will not happen in one night, like every financial decision that can be made, it needs time to grow before benefits can be retrieved. Therefore, whatever choice or decision you make to attain financial freedom, it important that you are able to exercise the virtue of patience to ensure that your finances and investments grow and develop to their full capacity. To make the topic or idea of financial independence appear more realistic, there are some levels and stages of growth peculiar to financial freedom that should bereligiously observed.These stages are subsequently discussed.

Stage 1: Establishment of an emergency fund. Many individuals claim to be interested in achieving financial freedom, however, their life is still determined based on the next salary or pay received. They do not have an emergency savings or savings of any sort, all their funds and money is lavishly spent the moment their company or corporation pays. These category of people are commonly referred to as individuals who survive or live paycheck to paycheck. This also includes paying off any credit card debt as it carries a large percentage of interest. However, this is the reality of most average Americans, this same category of people are also the same individuals that claim to be interested in achieving financial freedom or independence, some even claim that the entire financial freedom principle is unattainable. How can you achieve financial freedom when your debt continues to grow in its percentage of interest? Therefore, it is important to have a savings account where you are able to religiously contribute a percentage of you salary for unexpected expenses and to avoid money squandering.

Level 2: Retirement. At this stage an individual might have been able to gather or save enough money or funds to quit his job for a while or the long-run. The entire idea of financial freedom is to reach a stage where working or employment becomes a choice and not a necessity. However, the thought of quitting your job for the long-run might seem ridiculous or unreasonable because you are unable to for-see future needs. If the idea of full retirement is unreasonable for you, the step of taking a break from your job for a while is a nudge and a step in the right direction because that creates a familiar atmosphere with the feeling of retirement. It can be considered a preparation in advance.

Level 3: At this stage, individuals are expected to be financially stable, that is, the ability to indulge your major desires and still save a substantial amount of money. There is a feeling of relaxation and confidence when you can claim to be financially free and still be able to contribute to your saving plan. Therefore, any individual at this stage should be able to have a satisfactory lifestyle and still have a substantial amount of money to save at the end.

Level 4: Time. If you are an individual who has been able to enforce the early retirement scheme, then, you would realize that you have a large percentage of time to yourself. To invest in things that actually interest you not because you need financial assistance or support. Therefore, at this stage in your course to financial freedom, your time and schedule would become flexible. The flexibility in time and schedule is closely related to financial freedom. An individual in this stage is given the freedom to choose the activities and events that make up his day, also they are able to pursue tasks because of passion rather than compulsion, also, an individual becomes his own boss. There is the personal decision and shift in the program and time and events to involve your personal development, therefore, you can move things around your schedule until it fits your personal goals at that time. Every individual is familiar with the fact that one of the basics of financial freedom and independence is to ensure you pursue your passions, have more time for yourself and the important people to you without running out of funds to support yourself and your family while doing it. Any individual who claims to belong to this stage should be able to do this.

Level 5: A stable retirement plan. Individuals in their course to financial freedom must have been able to secure a retirement plan that would be able to withhold all your future expenses. Assuming you are an individual who belongs to the regular financial class, you need to ensure that you have earned enough to stabilize your life after retirement. Therefore, it is important that you have enough funds to actualize the lifestyle you desire after retirement. This is done by saving or investing in assets to ensure a long-term stream of income or dividends. Also, individuals who have been able to accumulate stable streams of passive income are also on the right path for an individual who plans to retire early.

Level 6: Financial freedom and independence. This is the final stage that the entire course, discipline and suggestions this book is designated to reach. It involves not having to stress about the profit of your passive income or the next paycheck and even the retirement plan you have laid out. It simply involves a stress or fret free life. This is the exclusivity that the financially free status offers. The attainment of this level usually means that you have more money than you will need to spend, most financially free people do not reach this status, they often stop at the fifth stage which is also a percentage of achievement. However, this level is usually occupied with individuals whose wealth is gotten from lotteries or inheritance or individuals who establish their own independently successful companies. Common examples of this founders are Bill Gates and Warren Buffet who have successfully attained financial freedom. Their businesses or companies are successful to the extent that if any of them decides to purchase yachts, planes and other unnecessary things, they would not succeed in exhausting the funds or wealth gathered. That is the true meaning of financial freedom.

Therefore, having highlighted the different levels of financial freedom, identify the stage you belong to and reflect if you are truly satisfied with it, if not, then ensure that you identify the things that would improve your financial growth to assist in achieving the specific level desired. Therefore, the definition of these steps is to encourage individuals to continue growing their wealth and to create an awareness that there is always more to sustain.

In affirming that the idea or principle of financial freedom and independence is actually a realistic information, it is necessary to share some testimonies of the financial freedom movement. Why exactly is this important? Because for some or many individuals, seeing is believing and in this case, they would have to read actual situation where financial freedom has been attained to eliminate the ideology that it is only a myth that can never be manifested. Hence, the importance of the following testimonies.

The first testimony to be considered would be that of Christina Yumul, who was able to move from San Diego to a different location which was in actual fact more expensive to afford- Maui, Hawaii. Alongside, moving she was able to settle her debt of $30,000 which was gained due to student loans and some excessive spending. This particular individual was able to prioritize, which was is one of the suggestions in this book, instead of the expensive lifestyle of partying to gain herself emotional satisfaction. This was replaced with hiking and hours on the beach which provided a similar level of relaxation. With the extra funds that she was able to save from doing these things, she was able to make minimal payments of her debt consistently. Apart from prioritizing, another choice that aided her was her application to have her paychecks sent as contributions to pay off her loans.As a result of this, she was not tempted to spend the salary or basic pay since it never really got to her. Christina was able to manage the small percentage of salary that remained by spending on necessities and not wants, also she ensured that she did not indulge herself in credit card loans as this would only create another percentage of debt to be settled by her. Therefore, she has been able to establish financial independence by paying her debt, establishing her own company and maintaining a healthy spending habit.

Also, a couple was able to pay off a mortgage that was supposed to be for 30 years in 6 years. 23 years earlier than the original year expected. This particular testimony was accounted for by Paige Hunter. This particular couple shared that the most beneficial part of attaining financial freedom is that that they are able to contribute to causes that actually interest them, and they are able to explore the world beyond what they know. The most interesting part of this story is that the Hunters have remained subscribed to the notifications of their mortgage despite the fact that it has been paid. Therefore, they get reminders every month for the mortgage and Paige described that happy endorphins are conjured in her because of this particular knowledge.

You might be wondering at this point "do I have to take a loan or be in debt before financial freedom is a possibility?" because the previous examples have started from the position of debt. The answer is "no", in fact, this next testimony would inform you that financial freedom is possible for any individual of any age or status. This is the case of Jessica Jabbar, a 27 year old advertising executive in New York City who claims to have saved six figures due to adherence to a strict saving regimen. According to her, she was able to attain this landmark by creating a strict and detailed budget for every sector of her life and also creating limits for everything she was involved. This individual also believes that now that she has made her first million, the most reasonable thing for her is to invest this funds. She believes that this funds as investment capital would do more profit to her financial status compared to when abandoned in a bank account.

For Sara Woznicki, after graduating from college she as ale to secure a job as a marketing specialist in Richmond, because his particular job had a low salary range, she struggled to pay rent and furnish her apartment. However, with assistance from her parents she was able to achieve some of her desires. However, after she attained a better payed job, her parents still rendered some assistance to, although it was minimal compared to the level they provided in her previous job. According to Sara, even after getting some percentage of responsibility due to the reduction of her parents' support, she was not exactly financially free until she was encouraged to get her own car insurance. The responsibility of the car insurance was solely on her and she could not testify or ascertain that she was financially until this point. With the newly established financial freedom and independence, she was able to save up and travel beyond her country for thee first time which is one of the benefits available or exclusive to a financially free status.

However, in some cases, you do not feel that you have attained financial freedom until some loans have been paid. In some cases, financial freedom creates the discipline that allows you to acquire only the necessities of life that would not have an adverse effect in your life. Therefore, financial freedom requires a discipline of wise budgeting, spending and saving. For Jill Bong and her husband, they were able to experience financial freedom when they admitted to the fact that some unnecessities had an adverse effect on their financial state. How did they dispose of these things? An example of the major expense which was unnecessary in their life was their high-loan payment house. They had a home in Colorado which was not contributing positively their finances, they decided to move to an affordable area and this had a remarkable effect on their finances. Due to this major change in their survival or living lifestyle, they were able to contribute better to other matters they had genuine interest and to invest in situations that would grow their finances. Because of this they have not been worried about their jobs since they have a reduced percentage of expenses and they are able to save more.

For individuals interested in the Financial Independence and Retire early movement, Dj Whiteside was able to testify on the effect of investment in stocks, cash and mutual funds on your early retirement plan. These particular couple had plans to retire early and had ensured they were consistent in their contribution to their retirement savings plan. At some point their decided to examine the worth of their retirement savings and identify if it would be sufficient for them in the long run. They realized that they had enough funds for their retirement years and even if they stopped contributing to their retirement savings, they would have a sufficientS amount of money due to heir investments and salary. According to them, financial freedom in relation to financial freedom or independence gives you confidence about your life post-retirement.

Therefore, based on the content and context of each of these individual stories, the concept of financial freedom is not one that can be generalized. Financial freedom has various individual meanings and interpretations for people in different situations. For Sara Woznicki, she did not regard herself as financially free until she was able to cut all financial ties with her parent. Therefore, different situations defineyour financial freedom. For some individuals, it is being able to buy gas or petrol for their vehicles without worry, others the ability to spend unlimited time with their family without feeling guilty for missing jobs. For most, it is simply being able to pursue the things they are passionate about.

Financial freedom is simply being the author of your own life by taking charge of your finances.

CPSIA information can be obtained
at www.ICGtesting.com
Printed in the USA
BVHW071553191020
591323BV00015B/2130

9 781801 095006